The Call of DIY

Benjamin Mee

THE CALL OF
DIY

The **Guardian**

ATLANTIC BOOKS
LONDON

Published in hardback in Great Britain in 2005 by Atlantic Books on behalf of Guardian Newspapers Ltd. Atlantic Books is an imprint of Grove Atlantic Ltd.

The Guardian is a registered trademark of the Guardian Media Group Plc. Guardian Books is an imprint of Guardian Newspapers Ltd.

ISBN 1 84354 425 3

A CIP record for this book is available from the British Library.

Photograph of Clint Eastwood courtesy of Rex; photograph of Gaudí's Casa Mila courtesy of Hulton Archive/Getty Images; picture of Isaac Newton courtesy of Time & Life/Getty Images; photograph of Blofeld courtesy of Rex/Everett Collection; photograph of Jean-Paul Sartre courtesy of Hulton Archive/Getty Images; photograph of Le Corbusier courtesy of Time & Life/Getty Images; picture of Aristotle courtesy of Time & Life/Getty Images; photograph of Professor E. O. Wilson courtesy of Jim Harrison; photograph of Winston Churchill courtesy of Hulton Archive/Getty Images.

10 9 8 7 6 5 4 3 2 1

Printed and bound in Slovenia
Text design by Katherine Carnegie

Atlantic Books
An imprint of Grove Atlantic Ltd
Ormond House
26–27 Boswell Street
London WC1N 3JZ

For the Bog Man

My thanks to . . .
Susie Steiner, Dominic Murphy, Stevie Brown
and Lisa Darnell at the *Guardian*, to Toby
Mundy, Alice Hunt and Louisa Joyner at Atlantic
Books, and to my wife Katherine who designed
this book and made it possible in so many ways.

contents

introduction

In Jack London's magnificent classic, *The Call of the Wild*, the hero, Buck, is snatched from a sun-kissed life of laziness in California and forced to endure the harsh ravages of the Alaskan goldrush instead. In adapting to this brutal Darwinian environment, Buck quickly becomes 'decivilized' and the primordial beast that lurks within him – and, London implies, in all of us – awakens.

OK, so Buck is actually a large dog and his circumstances are drastically more desperate than those in which I and most of my gentle readers find ourselves. But when we engage in the simple tasks of unblocking a sink, painting a wall, or feathering our nests in any way, we are answering a call exactly like the one that came to Buck as he stood at the edge of the forest with the safety of humans' fire at his back. The call of DIY and the call of the wild come from the same place. (Not the forest, via lumber yards: that would be facetious.) Our ancestry.

While the UK housing market boomed through the 1990s right up to the summer of 2004, spending on DIY steadily increased. When the market stuttered, spending on DIY increased again, with records broken at Christmas. One survey recently revealed that one pound in every twelve non-food pounds is spent on DIY, and that people are giving up holidays to do DIY instead – partly to increase the value of their homes, but also because it is increasingly seen as a rewarding pastime in its own right, elevated in popular perception from chore to satisfying leisure activity. For the first time, women are doing slightly more DIY than men, who are less likely to initiate projects and prefer to be directed by their more capable, sensible, and dynamic other halves, who drive the projects by 'nagging' and 'making lists'. A bit like life, really.

DIY is so popular that some have called it a new kind of religion, practised far more frequently, in the cathedral sheds of DIY superstores on Sundays, than any other religion in the UK, and probably the only thing spreading faster than radical Islam. But the call of DIY comes from much further back than that. Orang-utans build shelters particularly well, and our early hominid relative, *Homo habilis*, the tool user, began using stone tools around 2.5 million years ago. So DIY was born.

Initially hunting and building shelters were the main preoccupations of our ancestral DIYers, but things eventually progressed to matters of interior design, such as seating, tables, and cutlery. These became embellished for purposes of showing off, and the Arts and Crafts movement had arrived. But humble DIY continued, going from strength to strength to the point where it is consistently the largest and fastest-growing retail sector, worth £13.5 billion last year, or £257 per head for everyone in the UK over fifteen.

Which is quite strange, really. Surely, with the evolution of consciousness and the ability for self-reflection comes the ability to ask the question, 'Why DIY?' As builders emerged from the swamp (a process arguably still under way), why not pay a professional to do it? Particularly if you are relatively well off, it is uneconomical to spend time fiddling with screws and paint when you could pay someone else to do it better, yet even barristers on £400 per hour sometimes find it therapeutic to put up a shelf. Part of the allure of DIY is that it's a time sink, a way of storing your time so that a discerning audience will be able to appreciate it in the future. You never actually get your time back, but you can look at it as often as you like and see where it went, as well as referring to it in conversations for days afterwards until people get sick of hearing about it.

DIY is an itch you can never fully scratch, part of a never-ending continuum of activity that will occupy you while ever you have the will to modify your environment. Sometimes you can save money and take the time over the details that a professional might not; occasionally you may waste your time and materials, cause untold damage, and need a professional to help you out. But such frustrations are strewn along the route to greater knowledge, both of DIY and of yourself. DIY certainly confronts you early on with your fundamental laziness, petulance, and stupidity, which is a good start. And for all its sometimes nerdy image, DIY is quietly cool. Recently Brad Pitt admitted that he was 'pretty handy around the house', and the image of him in a tool-belt should bolster the morale of handymen and -women alike. But the best thing about answering the call of DIY is that afterwards you appreciate it even more when you hear the equally powerful call of the sofa, the takeaway dinner, and the remote control.

basics

The building blocks of DIY are not just the physical materials with which we work but also a series of attitudes, gradually acquired through experience. Thus, having a cup of tea first is a good attitude, while you assess the potential damage you are about to cause and weigh it up against the chances of your being able to put it right. If it seems viable, a good attitude towards adversity will also be useful, because every single thing will go wrong – certainly at first, but also, alarmingly, as you proceed. Above all, remember to be as lazy as you possibly can. If you feel you are exerting yourself in any way, you are probably doing something wrong.

the art of basic preparation

Basic preparation is where it all goes wrong, because people see preparation as something to be skipped through on the way to the real focus of the job: filling, painting, rejoicing at finishing, etc. No. No. No. Preparation is the focus of the job. Because proper preparation is so horrible that, once it's done, it's downhill from there on.

If you find yourself on a wobbly stool in the kitchen, dipping a paintbrush that's shedding bristles into gloss paint (which is bringing off the old paint in flakes because you haven't sanded properly), and the pasta needs attention because it's about to boil over, you've got it all wrong. For a start, you're having a takeaway tonight. The kitchen is a building site, and on building sites you eat takeaways.

Everything within a 3-metre arc of the affected area must be cleared, particularly things such as spice racks, already covered in years of congealed grime, or toasters, or anything that won't like a thick layer of dust. This is your time to claim the area. Nothing must distract you or get in the way. Wobbly stools have no part in your mission. Always use a stepladder or a strong table, cleared of domestic clutter and positioned squarely beneath your work area. Wear old clothes, and possibly goggles, against flakes of paint sent airborne by your ruthless use of the scraper, the weapon of choice for basic preparation. When it is done, and properly dusted, the sun comes out and the rest of the job can only go well. (And, of course, when you take preparation this seriously, procrastination is inevitable.)

how to store paint

Storing tins of paint can be a nightmare. I used to wake up screaming about it, until my good friend, Don, took over the responsibility when we worked together as (clueless) decorators. Locking up, he'd sometimes go back into the bowels of the building just to check that the tins were properly stacked.

We shared a cupboard with the cleaners, so the paint had to be secure or it meant a Jackson Pollock in the broom cupboard. But every rim on every tin was warped and buckled, making stacks that were more than two or three tins high dangerously wobbly. The trouble is that when you lever off the lid with a blunt chisel, or a 2p coin wedged into the rim and hit with a hammer, it frays the edges. Then it doesn't go back on properly, so you thump it with something heavy and buckle it even more. Repeat until lid is too frilled to secure purchase of 2p coin.

But I recently learned something that could have saved us those nightmares. Only open tins with the largest screwdriver you have (the screwdriver on a Swiss Army knife is good, too, because you tend to protect the tool as much as the lid). Then lightly smear the rim with Vaseline before replacing it precisely in position and squeezing it home with the heel of your hand, rather than thumping it with a hammer.

And you can build shelves from paint tins: a plank can be propped up with 5-litre tins for the bottom shelves, while 2.5-litre tins separate the higher tiers. Ideal for storing tools, bric-a-brac, and, as it happens, leftover tins of paint.

moving furniture

Whenever my dad asked us to help move furniture we knew we had to set aside a good three hours for the task – about twenty minutes to actually move the thing, and the rest of the time working on the plan. There was the measuring of all apertures – doors, windows, stairwells – through which the item was due to pass; the identification of potential trouble spots on the route and the formulation of a strategy for each; the allocation and briefing of personnel for every manoeuvre; the full rehearsal, involving walking the route; the oral examination of key personnel to ensure they understood their roles; and then, finally, the actual lifting.

Over the years, we developed a counter-strategy. Anything earmarked for moving would be miraculously relocated in his absence, 'as a surprise' for when he got back. Our method was to pick the thing up, run with it to the door, jostle it through, then jog on to the final destination. Sanity lies somewhere in the middle. Reconnaissance of the route and removing obstacles such as roller skates makes sense, and measuring can save a lot of time. Once, my dad discovered several of us wedged up a staircase with a wardrobe. 'It won't fit,' he said. 'I measured

it.' There are also energy-saving devices such as castors; sometimes it's easier to fit these than to lift something.

Taking reasonable care is the quickest method of all – our
way was still no faster than dad's: five minutes for moving and
two hours, fifty-five minutes to repair the damage.

the art of shovelling

I recently had to shovel rubble with Eric, a professional
labourer with arms of steel, a chest like a chest of drawers,
and a brain the size of a tree frog's. It was easy to see that he
relished the prospect of showing up a lily-livered keyboard-
tapper with woman's hands like myself. But Eric had one
major disadvantage: he was lazy.

But not quite as lazy as me. Every year, hundreds of people
injure themselves shovelling, often during autumn leaf clear-
ance or tidying up after DIY. That's because they're not lazy
enough. Not that you should leave leaves or rubble lying
around (though, if you can, you should), but the same incli-
nation to avoid expending energy will also prevent you from
straining yourself. Shovelling is all in the knees. Keep your

stance wide, so you can hold your back straight but still be low to the ground, and dangle your shovel between your legs as an orang-utan might.

As I said, Eric was perfect for it, but the critical difference between our techniques was that I swivelled my torso slightly, so my right elbow made contact with my right knee. This meant that the strength of my leg, rather than my arm, pushed the shovel forwards. Real idlers soon discover that, rather than actually moving your leg, you can just sink your weight on that side and your body mass sends your shovel skidding along with almost no effort. The momentum carries the load to your barrow, skip, or pile, allowing you to shift large amounts of debris without breaking sweat.

Poor Eric. He could have been good, but he didn't quite have what it takes.

in praise of gaffer tape

Gaffer tape, or duct tape as it is known in the USA, was invented by the American military in 1942 as a means of keeping ammunition boxes waterproof. Since then, it's been used in a bewildering array of applications, including the Apollo moon landings (mending the mudguard of the moon buggy), steadying Carrie Fisher's breasts during the filming of *Star Wars*, and holding together the broken handle of my hammer for the last eight years.

When I researched this column, I naively imagined I was among the first to recognize gaffer tape's unique contribution to humankind, but it already had a cult following. There are hundreds of websites packed with praise, tips on its uses, and photographs of things stuck together with it. People like it because it's incredibly strong yet easy to tear off the roll; it's waterproof and mends almost anything. You can even go micro: very thin strips, cut with a scalpel, can be applied to very small broken objects with tweezers.

Now in a range of colours, its youthful appeal is shown by a recent Internet poll where 60 per cent of voters wanted the name changed to 'gaffa'. Online, I also listened to an eleven-minute sermon linking duct tape (not gaffer) with the gospels. 'Bonding, bringing together, joining, mending; the purpose of the Bible – and of duct tape!' It's so useful that I decided to store my roll somewhere accessible. The back of my tool-cupboard door seemed a good place, so that every time I open it the roll is there. But what to secure it with? Well, that's obvious.

A hook.

how to clean tools

'Clean. Your. Sodding. Tools,' Mick used to say to me, in the nicest possible way. Actually, it wasn't that nice. He was my first guv'nor, a slip of a man in white overalls who felt an enormous professional responsibility to treat me like dirt, because that's what apprentices are. But he was also kind, occasionally tempering his instructions with explanations and guidance in The Way Of Decorating. And he was right about tools. They need to be clean so they are ready when you next need them, because that might be an emergency. If this sounds nerdy, think of Clint. He cleans his gun a lot for precisely this reason, and no one calls him 'speccy four-eyes'.

I thought of Mick recently when the lights went out at home and the tool I needed to fix them was a screwdriver that I'd left in a tin of gloss paint. It had hardened, though not all the way through, as I discovered, in the dark, in the cupboard under the stairs. Leaving tools dirty can jeopardize the next job; so knives used for filling, say, should be scraped thoroughly after use, and wire-brushed occasionally, or they will cause drags next time out. Paintbrushes can also be wire-brushed, to discourage the build-up of residues that will otherwise reappear in a critical topcoat further down the line. In short, if you don't clean everything every time you use it, then every time you go to your toolbox, or your cupboard under the stairs, you have to ask yourself the question, 'Do I feel lucky?'

Well, do you, punk?

Clint. No one
calls him a nerd.

the joy of demolition

Smashing things up is always fun, but there's a lot more to demolition than simply sanctioned vandalism. Of course, there's the simple pleasure of jemmying off an architrave and watching it spring helplessly off the wall and onto the floor, or thumping a sledgehammer into a brick wall until it succumbs to your inexorable onslaught, or even, for the uncouth, in putting a boot through a plasterboard partition (we've all done it, haven't we?).

But if demolition is enjoyable because it satisfies your appetite for destruction, how much more enjoyable it is when you know you're doing it properly. An enraged attack on an old Formica kitchen with a crowbar might sate your blood-lust for a moment, but it will also be largely ineffective and probably hurt your hands. Inevitably with violence, there will be flying shards of debris which risk injury and extra damage to repair afterwards. The way to get revenge on a much-hated kitchen is to dismantle it systematically, using a screwdriver to get the units off the wall (usually only held on with two screws), and the crowbar and club-hammer only as a last resort for things like a stubborn counter top.

There are other pleasures in demolition – say, unearthing beautiful original features, such as a hidden panelled staircase or an original fireplace. But, inevitably, the most enjoyable pleasure is the most primitive. Keeping a kitchen unit intact until you get it out to the skip means that you can then climb in with it and kick the crap out of it.

drilling

The first time I used a power drill I drilled a small hole in my forearm. It was my first day working for Big Peter Smith, and he was not impressed. 'Eh, Benjy,' he said in his strong Leeds accent, 'tha'z about as much use as a chocolate fireguard.' He put me onto filling the skip, and I didn't handle a drill again until years later when I put up my first shelf, which quickly became a crisis-management operation. I was tense, trying to get it over with, so I made every mistake possible. Gripping the drill tightly and using the wrong-sized carpentry bit on a masonry wall, it skidded a centimetre off its mark before creating a messy dent. Near enough, I thought, moving the other pencil marks a centimetre. I ground the surrounding area into a wide crater. No problem. Extra Rawlplugs. About seven. And some filler.

With hindsight, it's clear I was reacting to events, but basically I was afraid of the drill, which is, after all, a frightening object more like a gun than a tool: both have triggers, are vilely noisy, and can seriously damage walls and flesh. So the standard lecture from any sergeant major in any film about Vietnam applies: 'Do not be afraid of your power drill. Your power drill is like your girlfriend. Cradle your power drill, and squeeze the trigger gently.'

Sarge is right about a few other things, too. Planning should be military; secure the area if necessary. Safety first: goggles let you get in close, knowing that powdered brick won't spew into your eye. And keep your chuck key near by; reaching for the chuck key and not finding it is the power-drill equivalent of the dead man's click. Variable speed is very useful for screwdriving (think clutch control on a hill start); and something called the hammer-drill mode, I discovered, eases drilling into bricks.

Years later I showed my first shelves to Big Peter and learned another Yorkshire term for 'favoured employee': 'Eh, Benjy. Tha'z a wassock, tha knows.'

a stuck screw

A stuck screw is the kind of challenge that gets personal. Disproportionate amounts of effort and emotional energy are expended in undoing screws that could probably be forced or levered and the damage repaired in half the time. But it's worth it.

The way a screw takes you on is to get you gradually to commit all your weight and strength at an awkward (and, with hindsight, ill-considered) angle, and then suddenly give way. This often causes your face to come into contact with something hard, your knuckles to be skinned, and the head of the screw to be stripped. What was a stubborn screw becomes an embedded bit of metal, held in by the teeth of a thread that is impossible to turn. Very funny.

If you have a Dremel (a mini-grinder), you can grind a new slot into the head – though probably also into the surrounding wood, which may be a problem. Alternatively, lining up a screwdriver on the slot and then hitting it hard with a hammer is satisfying and may even loosen the thread in the wood. Possible lubricants include WD-40, soap, and detergent; and you could try turning it clockwise first – it won't be expecting that. Or grip the shaft of the screwdriver with pliers or mole grips (lockable pliers with rounded jaws) and commit all your weight (more judiciously this time).

If that doesn't work, No More Mr Nice Guy: heat the screw with a soldering iron until smoke comes out around the edges, hit it with a hammer, heat it, hit it, heat it, hit it, and then see if it wants to come out quietly.

decorating

Painting and decorating is one of the most accessible routes into DIY, a gateway activity that can lead to other things. But beware the stepladder effect, where one rung is never enough and jobs lead to other jobs that you wouldn't normally tackle but seeing as you're there you have a go. It's also a classic nest-feathering behaviour with relatively rapid gratification, particularly if you scrimp on the preparation. And decorating also has the advantage of masking more serious work that needs doing, hence the term 'papering over the cracks'. Or, indeed, filling and painting them when they clearly indicate a much deeper structural malaise.

stripping paint

Stripping paint can transform your woodwork from grotty to fabulous, but it will also have exactly the opposite effect on your mood. By the time you finish this attritional and upsetting task you will be depressed, so the first tip is: when you buy the dreaded Nitromors (the leading brand of paint stripper), buy yourself something nice to look forward to as well. Also buy reams of kitchen roll, a decent scraper, and plenty of white spirit and sandpaper.

Paint stripper blisters paint in seconds and will do the same to your skin. You'll know when you've spilt it on your skin from the instantaneous burning sensation. You'll soon learn to keep a bowl of water near by. A cardboard box is also a good idea, because you'll generate a lot of mess, and you can also clean your scraper on its lip. Dab on the paint stripper, wait for twenty minutes, apply more, then scrape it off. 'If paint remains, repeat process,' it says. And paint always remains. So repeat, repeat, and repeat, until you have completely lost heart. Then repeat a couple more times. To avoid gouging the scraper into the wood, press down on the blade with your free hand, while pushing up with your handle hand, to control the angle.

You can use a heat-gun, but these involve their own costly learning curve. Like a hairdryer on steroids, if the gun points at anything for more than a couple of seconds it sets it on fire. A friend has a paint-free but spectacularly charred window frame, and also ignited his roller blind. Heat-guns crack glass in an instant and send airborne particles of burning paint to start small fires in inconvenient places. On the up side, they can also be used for making instant toast and browning crèmes brûlées.

hanging wallpaper

These days, at least one wallpapered wall or alcove is essential if you want to be taken seriously, but wallpapering is a dastardly art to master.

Particularly difficult is papering round switches, doors, or radiators, most of which should be absent from your alcove. If not, choose a different alcove. Shelves should be taken down and put back up afterwards, which is generally easier than papering round them. A pasting table is a good investment, even if you don't intend to paper much in the future. It makes a good part of your DIY barricade, plus it folds up. And, if you ever want to set up a market stall selling home-made jam, it's there. A pasting brush, bucket, paste, sharp knife, and wallpaper are also required, as is a quiet mind. I think I might be wallpaper-phobic because I can happily apply paste to the back of the paper, but as soon as I pick it up I want to fling it away. This is not the way.

Hold a dry roll of paper against the wall and cut it 4 inches too long to allow for trimming at the top and bottom (complicated patterns need a surprising amount of extra paper to match up accurately, so be sure you have enough). Paste the paper, then press the top edge into position, smoothing out bubbles with a paperhanger's brush, which has soft, springy bristles. A soft broom will do, but make sure it hasn't been used for sweeping up soot (as mine had) or you'll have to go through the whole process again.

using a roller

If you think that watching paint dry is boring, then you're not doing it properly. The sick thrill of watching a second coat roll onto a recently plastered ceiling would be made illegal if only they knew. It's the middle of the night because you're well behind schedule (of course) and the second coat is drying patchily – everywhere streaks from the first coat are showing through. There's paint in your eyes and your heart is in your mouth and a voice inside you screams, 'Go back! Go back! Put on more paint.' But that is exactly what you must not do, or it will blister.

But that's the heady side of rollering. The other side is a businesslike tool that puts paint onto surfaces, fast. With a roller, a room can change colour in a day, and you don't even need dust sheets if you just roll nice and slowly, saving yourself for the giddy excitement of the drying stage. But before you even start rolling you have to do the 'cutting in', which is painting up to adjacent surfaces, like skirting boards or ceilings, or different-coloured walls. Some people recommend masking tape, but these people are wrong. Masking tape pulls off the paint that it's stuck to, it shreds when you try to peel it off, and – and – it lets paint leak underneath it anyway. Better to learn to cut in properly, with a 2-inch emulsion stripe around the bits that the roller can't reach.

Then you are ready to rock and roll. Pour out a tray of paint, wedge a broom handle into the back of your roller, and go for even, slightly overlapping stripes. Roller doodles will come back to haunt you during the difficult time halfway through the second coat, when you need to keep your head. It will look desperately bad before it looks better, with wallpaper sagging from the wall as it dries and yet everywhere crying out for more paint. Just remember, whatever you do, don't go back.

painting with gloss

Some people think gloss paint is smelly and difficult to apply. Others find it boring. I was shown how to use it by an artist with an obsessive compulsive disorder, so for me gloss is all about incredible patience, delayed gratification, and adrenalin.

To the usual shopping list of white spirit, primer, sandpaper, undercoat, and gloss paint, the artist added gaffer tape, plastic sheeting, more white spirit, and surgical gloves (theoretically for hygiene, but really because he liked wearing them). Before we were allowed anywhere near the paint, there was preparation to be done. We filled and sanded, sanded and filled, and sanded and sanded to a finish like porcelain. Sanding is the worst part of the job. For many people it's so bad it counts as a mini life-event. The best psychological strategy is to give up all hope of ever finishing and adjust to a new life of sanding, as if you are preparing for a long stretch in prison. Finally, we vacuumed the room with a soft-brush attachment, wiped every surface with white spirit and sealed the room with plastic sheeting and gaffer tape – with us on the inside. 'This is now a Dust-Free Zone,' the artist declared, using up valuable oxygen. 'Nothing comes in or out.'

If you're planning to put aside a weekend for glossing, put aside two. Try to get close to the dust-free, porcelain state during the first two days, then spend all week dreaming of dolloping on the paint. We used a separate primer and undercoat (you can buy them combined), then an extra undercoat and two coats of gloss. Between each coat we sanded, vacuumed the room, and wiped with white spirit. Finally, it was time for the last coat of gloss – and, trust me, there was a lot riding on this. Use a good brush to get rid of streaks. You don't have much time to correct mistakes on gloss before it dries, so keep edges 'live' by going over them repeatedly.

Although eccentric, the artist was right about one thing: dust is the enemy of gloss. Prepare well. But don't go mad. You can probably do without the surgical gloves.

painting wooden floors

Fortunately for those seeking to change the colour of their floors, there is floor paint. Unfortunately, it seems to come only in colours that you would not want on your floor. A typical colour range is dark green, slate grey, and tile red, otherwise known as school, prison, and garage. Even if this were your career trajectory, you wouldn't want to be reminded of it in your own living room.

Because of its commercial applications, floor paint also tends to be massively overspecified for your needs. Even tins from the humblest hardware shop claim resistance to oil, petrol, kerosene, isopropyl alcohol (what about red wine?), and hydrochloric acid – though specifically not hydrogen peroxide, so no home hair-bleaching. Suggested uses are 'concrete and wooden areas such as garages, warehouses, workshops, factories, and aircraft hangars'.

But most living-room floors don't get significantly greater wear than stockinged feet and a soft brush sweeping up the Pringle crumbs from the night before. So forget floor paint and just use the normal topcoat of your choice, in any finish or colour. First, sand lightly. Don't get into proper floor sanding. Scrape off big, loose splinters with a filling knife, but don't fill unless you have to: just paint more thickly over blemishes; it's amazing what a few thick coats can hide. Use an acrylic primer/undercoat applied liberally, followed by two or, for the conscientious, three coats of the topcoat.

I used a drab-green eggshell, which was nice. The only disadvantage is I have to park the Lear jet in the garage.

laying mosaic tiles

They laughed at Antonio Gaudí when he began putting up organic, often tiled, curvy buildings around Barcelona, and they laughed at me when I did my curvy shower. But there, I

suppose, the similarity ends. Gaudí was a great genius able to express himself on a city-wide scale, whereas I just couldn't be bothered to smooth out the bathroom wall before tiling it.

My downfall was realizing that those mosaic tiles that come in strips can be laid over uneven surfaces. So, rather than fight my wall's natural bumpiness, I decided to go with it. Instead of replastering, I just hacked out the loosest stuff and filled in with plaster, applied over a strip of plasterer's reinforcing wire (like narrow-gauge chicken wire) flexed across the bends. Which is where the problems started.

Mosaic tile sheets are supposed to be laid like ordinary tiles, but ordinary tiles aren't usually laid over bends. On the flat bits, the sheets sank into the adhesive easily and the mesh backing held each little tile the requisite distance apart. But on the bends it pushed them far too close together and I had to cut some sheets into strips to get the distance right.

Gaudí's curves: intentional, not just expedient.

No one said making great works of art would be easy. Grouted, it looks great and, though it may never be declared a World Heritage site, I'm sure Gaudí would have approved. And if anyone from UNESCO is reading, you can pop round for a shower any time.

painting over a damp patch

Denial is good, particularly when dealing with damp. It might have serious implications if left untreated, but with damp the root causes are often too terrible even to contemplate. Penetrating damp could be caused by something as simple as a cracked downpipe, but may be as bad as a bridged wall cavity, requiring significant surgery to the fabric of the building. Rising damp is usually worse, caused by problems with your damp-proof course or membrane, which you don't want to think about. Far better to paint over the problem and walk away.

Fortunately, there is a company that aids and abets damp denial: Johnstone's. They produce something called damp-proof paint. Unperturbed by moisture, it contains a 'water-reactive agent' (basically concrete) which gets stronger the wetter it gets. Within reason. It comes in white but can be painted over with pigmented breathable masonry paint. (One problem: it won't go over mould, which should be treated first.) Slap it on nice and thick, because it's doing you a big favour.

To be fair to Johnstone's, they stress that their product 'does not remove the need to repair any structural faults which allow water to penetrate the wall'. But for the likes of you and me, that's an open invitation to abuse. Faced with getting a grip on ourselves and the root cause, or getting a tub of Häagen-Dazs and a DVD and repainting every few months (and ultimately every few weeks until we manage to sell the place), we're helpless.

painting a radiator

Painting an old-fashioned radiator is a bit like restoring an old steam train: it brings you into contact with another age. Modern reproduction column radiators have names such as Schoolhouse and Church Hall for those who want to remember a simpler time of being able to see your breath while warming your bottom. Modern designers have also produced some racier versions of what is essentially a hot pipe with fins. What all column radiators have in common is that they allow heated water to lose heat through the radiator's large surface area. They also defy conventional paintbrushes to delve into their inner recesses.

What you need is the painting and decorating equivalent of a gun that shoots round corners. Hamilton Acorn, makers of fine brushes since 1746, have introduced (through B&Q) a range of curved brushes with bristles that taper to a point. These delve perfectly into your recesses and complement the beauty of the object you're painting. Start from the inside of each panel or column and work outwards, sanding, under-coating and glossing, taking time to reflect on the physics of the whole surface area—heat loss thing: how eddying air currents (probably predictable through fractals) imperfectly but inevitably heat the room.

Which brings you on to pondering the somewhat trying issue of old-fashioned column radiator maintenance. Which is why next time I'm definitely going for underfloor heating.

carpentry

Carpentry is probably one of the oldest human and, indeed, hominid skills, dating back at least to *Homo habilis* approximately 2.5 million years ago, so is it any wonder that we sometimes get the urge to make things out of wood? Wood has always been to hand – used as a weapon, for gathering food, and now, incredibly, in planed standard sizes for shelving. Our relationship with plants is extraordinary, but our reliance on harvesting trees with ever more sophistication was probably an engine of our evolution and still underpins much of our society. But try telling them that at the timber merchant's and they don't want to know.

fitting a floating shelf

A floating shelf is one that seems to hover against the wall with no visible means of support. When I first saw one, I behaved like a dog looking in a mirror for the first time and tried to peer round the back. With no brackets, it seemed like a plank glued to the wall; but closer inspection revealed it to be a hollow box hiding jiggery-pokery.

For years, I wondered how it was done, and how to make one myself. It obviously involved some sort of rod system, embedded deep into the wall to support the weight of the shelf. But ideally, to go into masonry, one end of the rod should have a screw thread for a Rawlplug. And then I discovered the 'concealed fixing shelf bracket', which is exactly that: a 7-inch rod with a screw thread at the wall end and 4 inches of smooth steel bar at the other, designed to slot into a hole drilled into your thick bit of wood. The smooth end even has a couple of bits of rubber on it which can be jiggled around to make sure the shelf will be level. (I wish I'd known that before I put up mine.)

Drilling edge-on into wood is tricky; don't grip the wood between your thighs, as a power drill could definitely access your femoral artery, which you don't want. My 'concealed brackets' stuck out of the holes I'd drilled at two quite different angles. No problem, I thought: I can just drill into the wall at the same two odd angles and the shelf will be level! Astonishingly, this plan failed, leaving my shelf floating at about 70°, rather than 90°, to the bathroom wall. Stops the toothpaste from rolling off, though.

making a bird table

The British appetite for bird tables has altered the migration patterns of several European bird species. After all, why fly to Marrakesh for the winter when you can live it up in East Cheam? Bird tables are traditionally boxy-looking and bought from garden centres, but you can make a much nicer one yourself for next to nothing. I happen to be living in the countryside at the moment, and while out walking I found a forked branch that spoke to me.

'Bird table,' it said, which was strange because I'm not particularly interested in birds. But, stripped of bark and trimmed to manageable proportions with a garden saw, it soon began to resemble a piece of bona fide garden furniture. One of the tines of the fork also had a fork in it, which gave me three prongs to work with. Branches such as this are not hard to find; they are, quite literally, lying on the ground in parks. When the three tines are cut to the same height they provide a stable platform for your bird-table top. I used a large shard of 6-millimetre-thick glass, which, as luck would have it, I had foraged from a skip only six and a half years before. After I'd 'grozed' (gnawed) around the edge with pliers to make it safe, it wedged nicely into some 6-millimetre slots cut about 2 inches down from the top of each tine.

I sharpened the other end of the branch into a stake and stuck it into the ground in a prominent place where I can watch the birds skidding around on the glass as they land. No free lunch, birdies.

repairing skirting boards

Skirting boards seem sacrosanct – a permanent fixture put there by grown ups, which mere DIYers tamper with at their peril. Not so. Skirtings are often wedged into place by morons as an afterthought. I've seen one kicked into position with a steel-toecapped boot, but once it was there it looked inviolable. I'm here to tell you that, if you want to, you can tamper with your skirting board. It is your right.

Quite often, due to alterations and shoddy workmanship over time, skirtings become mismatched, so that three walls are 1 foot high with ornate mouldings, while the fourth bears a 3-inch strip of pine. Take a drawing of your moulding to the timber merchant's and you will be surprised how easily he can match it, either off the shelf or by making up a composite. Prize the old board away from the wall with a crowbar – which is quite cathartic, actually. For long pieces that are wedged in at both ends, lever the middle away from the wall, hold it there with bits of two-by-one, then saw it in half. Then you can pull the two ends away. Even posh skirtings can be nailed (or kicked) into masonry or stud walls, or you can use screws and Rawlplugs.

I recently fitted a sliding door where there had been a hinged one, which involved removing the architrave and left a 6-inch gap in the skirting. Could I be bothered to walk to the timber merchant's with my little drawing? No, I couldn't. Not when I could lie down with a tub of mildly intoxicating two-part wood filler, watch the telly, and sculpt in the gap with a putty knife instead.

repairing window sills

As the days draw in and the evenings get colder, spare a thought for your window sill, suffering in silence out there on the other side of the glass. A window sill sits in one of the most vulnerable positions on the outside of the house, exposed to the sun and to all the rain that hits the window and the wall above it and cascades across this water-absorbent piece of wood. Chances are that no one's given this neglected length of timber a second thought for a decade, and an exploratory prod with a screwdriver will punch through a thin crust of paint into fibrous mush underneath. This is wet rot, and, if you're lucky, it will have consumed less than a third of the sill. Any more than that and you'd better get rid of it.

If you're bent on repair, think of it as an opportunity to test the mettle of your local hardware-shop browncoat, and ask for a three-sided shavehook (or a combination shavehook). This is a particularly vicious scraper and ideal for gouging out wet rot. Thoroughly dig out all the mush (you're being cruel to be kind). Take it right back to the dry hardwood underneath, until the blade makes a truly terrible fingernails-on-blackboard screech.

Next, you need to eradicate all traces of wet rot, using wet rot eradicator, which comes in tins from your local DIY superstore. You'll find it near the wood hardener and wood filler, which you will also need. Make sure you get a two-part filler, as it forms a stronger chemical bond. Paint on the eradicator. When dry, paint on the hardener. Then mix the filler and reconstruct your sill. My tin of filler said 'low odour – pleasant to use', which was a double lie. After you've sanded and painted it, you will only have eyes for your window sill for a few days. And then you can forget all about it for another ten years.

fitting a cat flap

It is widely believed that Isaac Newton invented the cat flap. As the great man sat grappling with some of the most complex thoughts in history, he was occasionally disturbed by having to put the cat out. Newton turned his enormous brain to the problem for a nanosecond, came up with the cat flap, and got back to redrawing the universe.

These days you can get cat flaps for doors, windows, and outer walls, which all come with a template to draw around. In doors, drill holes at points around your template and cut out the shape with a jigsaw; or, for the non-electrically inclined, use a padsaw (about £10), which cuts curves in wood. Be careful not to make the hole bigger than the flap; sounds obvious, but it happens. The two halves of the cat flap then simply clip together and screw into place.

With glass, it's 90 per cent certain you'll break the pane if

Newton's early cat-flap experiments were unsuccessful, until he hit upon the ground-level, cat-sized portal which is still in use today.

you try it yourself, but there's no harm in trying – either way, you'll end up at the glazier's. Score around your template in one motion with a glass cutter, without overlapping at the join, then score cross-hatches inside. Tap around the shape until the crack goes all the way through, then repeat on the cross-hatches. It'll never work.

For walls, hammer-drill your holes, then chip out the brick with a cold chisel, a heavy finger of metal about an inch wide. Wall-mounted cat flaps are not always lined, so line the tunnel with plywood. My dad uses lino (which the cat now prefers to her basket). Owners of bullied cats should go electromagnetic, so the flap opens only for a special cat collar. It is satisfying to hear Tiddles hurtle into the kitchen, followed by the thud of the bully against the shut flap, learning that action and reaction are equal and opposite.

putting in a letter box

I've been staying somewhere rural, and although it's nice to walk down to the gate in the morning to pick up wet letters from a leaky box at the end of the drive, I think on balance

I'd prefer to give the benefit of the walk to the postman and have dry letters delivered inside the house. There are probably people who would recommend taking the door off its hinges and laying it across a couple of trestles so that you can work on it horizontally, but I took the easier option of leaving the door in place and simply using my special rotating neck and arm joints to adjust to the vertical plane.

Positioning is important with a letter box. Could someone cunning reach the latch with a bent coat-hanger? Or, if you live in an angling community, what could they do with a fishing rod? Chiswick police issue the following crime prevention information regarding letter boxes: 'Do not leave any property on display in the hallway which can be fished out through the letter box. Consider installing a letter-box guard.' While you're considering, mark out your rectangle, drill a pilot hole in each corner, unleash a jigsaw, and join the dots. Screw your letter-box flap into place, and you're ready for the Christmas rush of bills and final reminders.

Last week, from the warmth of my bed, I watched the postman trudge, bent against the rain, up to the house. I listened to the unfamiliar clatter of the new letter box and rushed downstairs to find . . . an overdue parking ticket reminder.

making a hobby horse

Some days I get woken with a metal truck in the face, so I thought I'd make my toddler a hobby horse to play with instead. All you need is a knackered broom, some 6-millimetre plywood, and a jigsaw. If you don't have a jigsaw, I'd recommend buying one, although purists and paupers may prefer a £10 hand-held box saw, which will do the same job but with a lot more hard work. Draw a horse head on paper first, cut it out, and transfer it to the plywood. If you're bad at drawing, copy one from a chess set. The secret of using a jigsaw is to go about as fast as if you were writing with icing. Cut a slot the same width as your handle into the plywood, and glue it in later.

But first, sand off the splinters and paint your horse's head. You can really go to town with details such as a woollen mane and leather ears, or you can think, 'What the hell, the kid's visual sense works on a template system which supplies an idealized notion of "hobby horse" anyway,' and slap on a coat of grey paint with a black dot for an eye. Old handbag straps tacked to the mouth area make good bridles, especially the detachable ones with metal fittings, but make sure that you get permission from a grown-up first.

And how do you avoid getting hit in the face with it in the morning? Simple. Hobby horses live outside in the hobby-horse stable, or shed, as it's otherwise known. Now go and buy a new broom handle to replace the one you've nicked; and really, really, do get permission for using those handbag straps, or it's just not worth the hassle afterwards, I can tell you.

fitting a serving hatch

If there wasn't a serving hatch in *Abigail's Party*, there should have been. In the 1970s, hatches were up there with beige Austin Princesses, and featured in sitcoms of the time so that lines such as 'Ooh George' and 'I'm free' could be delivered through them with extra comedy value. But they're also handy for passing things (traditionally food) between rooms, and for encouraging other forms of inter-room communication, such as eavesdropping while appearing to be cooking.

You can put hatches into brick walls, even supporting brick walls; but this needs much planning, so leave it for another time (like never). Stud walls can be load-bearing, too.

If in doubt, don't forget: a structural engineer's quote is cheaper than a collapsed building. If, perchance, a non-supporting stud wall divides your kitchen and eating area, putting in a hatch is an afternoon's work. Bash a hole where you want it to be, using a claw hammer. Then measure up properly around the damage. Ideally, your hatch will be determined by where the studs (wooden supports) lie in your wall. The fewer studs you cut, the stronger the hatch will be (plus, it's less work). Ideally, cut just one stud, then saw the plasterboard (using a £10 drywall saw) into a neat square as far as the studs on either side. Line it with wood, choose an architrave, then decide on double-hinged, concertina, or sliding doors.

And then, whenever you're in the kitchen doing prawn cocktails for six, you will still be able to hear Demis Roussos playing in the lounge.

plumbing

Plumbing is something that really does separate man from beast. Never mind arguments about abstract thought, theory of mind, and use of symbols and language – the ability to flush away your poo is the cornerstone of civilization. Which somehow leaves all those who deal with it tainted with the bestial, which is why plumbing is perceived as unclean and plumbers are the lowest caste of the building trade. Plumbers suffer unjustly from this association with human waste, as plumbing is relatively clean, skilled work requiring some thought and planning. Which is why you're often better off doing it yourself.

burst pipes

A burst pipe can soon become a calamity of unimaginable proportions. One minute you're tapping a nail into a wall, the next there's a jet of mains-pressure water shooting into your eye. Within seconds, the carpet, hi-fi, and telly are ruined and a short circuit has started a small fire in the loft. If you can't find the stopcock, this is only the start, with many more rooms to be ruined and, for flat dwellers, not all of them your own (insurance up to date, is it?).

Another common cause of burst pipes is freezing in winter. In such circumstances, my plan A is to crumple into a sobbing heap until the emergency services arrive and lead me away in a blanket. Plan B is to turn off the mains at the stopcock, cut a 6-inch length of garden hose, slit it length-ways, and wrap it around the hole, binding it tightly with wire or butterfly clips. I'm now on plan C, which means planning ahead by ordering a 'pipe repair tape kit' from www.screwfix.com, which includes a fibreglass tape that sets hard when it comes in contact with water for a temporary fix. On the packet it says it can be used underwater, so if things get really bad you can swim down and fix it in a couple of deep breaths. More permanent is the 'push fit pipe repair': a short flexible hose with plastic fittings on each end. Saw out the burst section and slot it into the gap – easier than finding a sympathetic plumber in your soggy Yellow Pages.

Plan C means I'm ready for anything. Unless disaster strikes while I'm on holiday, in which case I'll revert to plan A on my return.

changing taps

Our new tap is the best thing to happen to our kitchen since the extractor fan arrived. Between them, tap and fan have added 'a couple of thou' to the value of the kitchen, according to an estate agent. We had set our sights on an outrageous single pillar tap that looked like a twenty-third-century fire hydrant. Just in time I realized that it was metric and our present tap was imperial, so the pipes would have been the wrong size.

That's if you can get the old tap off without cracking the sink. The worst-case scenario is a cracked sink and the pipework needs replacing. I contacted the Bathroom Association (www.bathroom-association.org.uk) who told me that the best-case scenario is to simply change the tap tops. 'Say you've got peach tiles (how did they know?); just get peach tops to match.' (Nice.)

Changing tap tops means replacing the hot and cold cross-tops leaving the base, plumbing, and spout in place. I unscrewed the body of the tap with an adjustable spanner, jiggled the fiddly bits holding the washer in place, and tightened it all up. Top tip: while unscrewing the body of the tap, steady the spout with adjustable pliers, but wrap a rag round it first or you'll gouge huge, permanent scratches into the chrome. And don't forget to turn the water off first. Then, hey presto. Goodbye manky encrusted cross-tops, hello new easy-action lever. Not a twenty-third-century fire hydrant perhaps, more sort of techno-organic, hybrid chic.

Now, what am I going to do with that two grand?

unblocking a sink

Even though most of my follicles shed their loads down the plughole long ago, somehow unblocking the sink is my job.

Nine times out of ten, a quick scratch around with the fingernails does the trick. Otherwise, you'll need a plunger.

The plunger is a wonderful device, more primitive than a mangle, cheaper than a pint of beer, and well worth the investment. Purists smear Vaseline round the rim to make an airtight seal; but as long as you block the overflow with a wet cloth while you plunge (ten to twenty times should do it), most domestic blockages will be slooshed into the sewers where they belong.

If the water still doesn't drain, you'll have to meet The Blockage head on. Get a bucket, some rubber gloves, and maybe a breathing mask. Goggles too, for the really squeamish (imagine getting splashed in the eye!). Sinks are thoughtfully fitted with a U-bend pipe, or trap, which stops earrings from going the way of other waste. In it, you hope, is The Blockage. Don't panic. With a bucket in place it can't go too badly wrong. Sometimes there is an access cap on the bottom of the U-bend, or you might have to unscrew the whole thing. Either way, you may need a wrench.

If the U-bend is empty, you'll have to go into the next bit of piping (via another access cap) and poke around for slime with a bent coat-hanger. Nice. Still, count yourself lucky if you drag out something revolting at this stage. If you don't, it does not augur well. It augurs an auger. An auger is a long-distance whisk with teeth: a handle and a length of flexible steel ending in swirling fangs for slicing into slimy blockages, like a robo-tapeworm. Not for the faint-hearted. And don't forget to clean those teeth thoroughly afterwards.

Filthy Pete

The last time we used a plumber, Filthy Pete, his personal hygiene was so bad we'd have paid him £80 just to go away. But the tap kept on dripping. The cure was either a simple washer, or a simple washer plus £80 plus Filthy Pete. So I got hold of a flat-headed spanner, a small screwdriver, and some mole grips. Then I waited five and a half years for the drip to really get to me before I decided to find the stopcock. Always know where your stopcock is: it looks like a frilly doorknob and stops the water supply.

On round-headed taps, the knob should just pull off. On a cross-top tap, beneath the plastic hot or cold disc is the grub screw (small, headless, looks like a larva), holding on the head of the tap. Grub screws love to jump down plugholes, so make sure you put the plug in. Take off the cross-top and unscrew the bell-shaped cover. If it's stubborn, wrap it round with a cloth and mole-grip it off. At the bottom of the tap mechanism is a nut (usually 13/16 inch, so get the right-sized spanner). But don't pile in with your spanner: grip the body of the tap with the mole grips while undoing the nut or you may crack the bath or the connecting pipe. With the tap gone, you'll see a washer, a rubber disc the size of a penny, sitting in a shallow dish. Then just replace the washer (priced 30p!). The reassembling process is just a matter of retracing your steps.

Top tip: plumbing is high risk. One mistake and you'll have to explain to your neighbour why it's raining in his hall, so have the number of a good back-up ready. (Visit www.registeredplumber.com. Filthy Pete isn't a member. I checked.)

unblocking a toilet

There comes a time in everyone's life when the buck stops with you. You can't defer to a responsible adult because you are that adult. You are the one who has to unblock the toilet.

Happily, the few toilet blockages I have attended have always been in the presence of people clearly far more responsible than myself. Dale Courtman of the Institute of Plumbing has unblocked more toilets than he'd care to remember. 'It's a nasty business,' he warns. 'Call a plumber.' Publicity trip over, Dale confides: 'In thirty years of plumbing, the old-fashioned plunger has never let me down. Mine wasn't the inverted cup shape. Just a flat disc on a handle.' Another kind of toilet plunger is the Cooper's plunger, Mr Cooper having been keen to be remembered for a stick with a funny-shaped rubber head which bulges around the U-bend when you shove it down the toilet. In the unlikely but horrible event that these aren't sufficient, you need to hire an auger, a piece of flexible hose with a handle at one end and swirling alien teeth on the other. These teeth mince the most vile blockages, but give the toilet a few flushes before you pull it out in case there's anything stuck between them. If the blockage is further down the pipe, you'll have to hire drain rods, which screw together like a chimney-sweep's brush.

But if it hasn't happened to Dale in thirty years, it's unlikely you'll need more than the trusty plunger. Dale's drill is simple: 'Take a deep breath and get both hands on the plunger. Insert it into the toilet and give it twenty or thirty good solid plunges, making sure you've got plenty of rags or old towels handy for the mess. Wear rubber gloves and old clothes. It's disgusting. God, I'm glad I don't do that any more.'

replacing a central heating timer

If, like me, you are one of those people who has trouble programming a video, often loitering before going out so you can press Rec/Play (the only way you really know for sure), then you may also be stuck when it comes to the mechanical timer on your central heating. This is essentially intermediate technology: a simple plastic wheel rotating through a single revolution every twenty-four hours. Little spokes on the wheel correspond with the hours of the day, and you can press them down or pull them up to set the times for the heating to come on and go off.

The spokes can be fiddly, but if you try to be clever (as I obviously did) and use a Swiss Army knife, they can snap off and leave you fairly committed to having the heating coming on at 5 a.m. It was time for a change, so the plumbers' merchant's sold me a top-of-the-range digital number that boasts vastly improved 'functionality'. That was what I was afraid of.

Apparently, this new fella would just wire right in, provided my old timer had what's called a 'backplate'. A backplate is a metal box embedded in the wall, like the one you find behind a light switch or plug socket, and I am rarely as pleased as I was when I saw the inside of mine in the hall. I unscrewed the old timer, wired in the new one with three wires, and, with a dab of filler, joined the twenty-first century.

Three temperature options at different times of the day, a different programme for every day of the week, and, of course, the most important button: manual override.

bleeding a radiator

Bleeding radiators isn't real plumbing. It's like letting the wind out of a mechanical cow. Just as a cow's four stomachs lead to its prodigious gas output, your central heating can get air trapped too. Water expands when heated, so every time your boiler comes on, the water in the radiators takes up more room than it did a minute ago (that's why you have an expansion tank in the loft for it to expand into). When it contracts again, it can suck in air. Air also gets in through small leaks (surprisingly common, particularly around radiator valves) during expansion and contraction. A classic symptom of trapped air is if your radiators don't get warm at the top. You may also hear ruminant-style gurglings. Get a radiator key. Locate the bleed nipple, or valve shank, usually on a top corner of the radiator, and try your key. Now go back and buy one the right size (they're not standardized). Standing by with a mug for catching water and an old towel just in case, slot in your key. Turn it a quarter of a turn anticlockwise; no more, or you'll get covered in brown stuff. Leave the air leak to flow out (this may take some time) until a spit of water begins, then shut it off. Plumbers, apparently, then give it another quick quarter turn. That's £50 you've saved.

If you need to bleed your radiators more than once every year or two you could have Expansion Tank Valve Grief, which should be addressed sooner rather than later because air in the system means rust. Rust is cholesterol for central heating, and you don't want the old girl to get that, as it can lead to major central heating surgery.

plumbing in a washing machine

I wasn't confident about this, though I've done it once or twice before. The first time, I was guided by an elderly lady for whom I'd just hefted the washing machine into place. She knew how to do it and talked me through each step without us ever having to acknowledge my ignorance. The other time – for a younger, less clued-up lady – it didn't work out, for some technical reason. So when my own white goods came inching up the stairs, I was pretty nervous about interfacing my washing machine with its plumbing. But it turns out to be an absolute doddle.

The plumber left a hot and a cold water supply pipe, just as he said he would, each with a colour-coded plastic valve. The washing machine came with similarly colour-coded plastic pipework, which just so happens to screw perfectly into the plumber's valves. The plumber recommended tightening these plastic fittings with adjustable pliers before turning on the valves. There's a flexible hose for the waste water, which slots into the waste pipe (also left by the plumber), connected by a 'spigot' which juts out of the waste pipe under the sink. And, er, that's it. Almost. Usually, there are some security bolts to hold the drum in place while in transit. You absolutely must undo these before you turn it on, or, on the first spin cycle, your brand new Bosch will start fighting itself in the middle of your kitchen.

So, just heave the machine out, disconnect the bolts, and start all over again. Simple.

fixing a ballcock

One of my proudest moments was fixing the only toilet at a busy party. The cross-legged queue outside the door lit up with that special and rare affection reserved for facilitators of mass bladder release. I, however, came away with a more permanent appreciation and awe of the ballcock, a simple mechanism by which physics thwarts the ambitions of mains water to flood the bathroom.

After a flush, as the water level inside the cistern rises, it inexorably brings about its own nemesis by floating a plastic ball attached to an arm that gradually plugs the supply. If it's dripping, it may be a good idea to replace it, but study your ballcock well before setting out for the plumbers' merchant's, or the men in brown coats will take you apart like Ronnie Barker in *Open All Hours*. 'Bottom-entry ballcock, is it, sir?' (pause for laughter). 'Or slimline side-entry?'

I phoned Dale Courtman, technical director of the Institute of Plumbing, so technically Britain's top plumber. 'There should be an isolating valve on your toilet,' says Dale. 'It may look like a tap, or have a small screw head which you turn across the flow to shut it off. Then flush and sponge out the cistern.' Bottom- or side-entry, either will yield to an adjustable spanner, and then you can take the whole offending mechanism to meet the men with the Biros in their top pockets. 'The difficulty comes with retracing your steps,' says Dale. 'Tightening up the nuts enough to stop it leaking, but not so much that you strip the threads. I'd recommend www.registeredplumber.com.'

But I'd definitely recommend getting to know your ballcock.

electrics

With over 750 injuries and ten deaths each year in the UK from faulty wiring and poorly fitted electrical equipment, it is probably for the best that the government has introduced new regulations prohibiting much electrical work in the home. None of the following items contravenes the new regulations – not that it would make much difference. Surveys show that 60 per cent of the public haven't heard of the legislation, and 60 per cent also say it wouldn't stop them from doing work themselves or getting other unqualified people to do it. But don't.

how to wire a plug

'Brown is hot, blue is not, green and yellow earths the lot.' This was the government-sponsored slogan taught to me in school after the changeover from the old 'red is hot, black is not' system. This switch to a more complicated system, with the need to invent a dodgy slogan to explain it, helped consolidate in me a scepticism about the people who think up these things. Brown is live because the second letter is R and it goes to the Right terminal of the plug. Blue is neutral because the second letter is L and neutral goes to the Left. 'Why not red for live, Miss?' I asked. 'Red actually begins with R, plus everybody already knows it's dangerous. And surely earth should be brown, because brown is the colour of earth?' My recommendations went unheeded, but the dodgy slogan still rattles in my head.

The trickiest bit is stripping the rubber insulation with a Stanley knife without cutting the copper wire. This can be avoided by investing in proper wire strippers. Expose 1 centimetre of bare copper, twisted and doubled up to make a neat nub which slots snugly into the terminal. Make the earth wire slightly longer than the others, so that when the cable is yanked out of the plug, it's the last to come out. Tighten the terminal screws to ensure a good contact, taking care that the cable passes through the cord clamp. Screw the back onto the plug, and you are ready to tap into the National Grid.

Slogans aside, I was pleased to be empowered by plug wiring, which soon enabled me to turn on, tune in, and drop out.

how to change a light bulb

Stretched out, the filament of a 60-watt light bulb would be 2 metres long. It would also be a lot harder to light up. Illumination depends on fast-moving electrons crashing into static molecules in the filament, which is much more easily achieved if the filament is very thin and very tightly coiled, which also helps it to fit into the bulb. All those subatomic collisions create a temperature of 2200ºC (and light), so it's no wonder that bulbs that are regularly subjected to vibrations suffer. This is why you change the hall light, next to the slamming front door and underneath the thunderous landing, three times more frequently than the landing light. The average bulb life of 900 hours can also be halved by dust, so dust your bulbs for greater efficiency. Top tip: if you are in the bath when the bathroom light goes and you can reach a replacement bulb and put it in without getting out of the bath – don't.

And so, on to the mandatory light-bulb jokes: How many bloggers does it take to screw in a light bulb? Dude, light bulbs are totally old media; we can now download photons directly from the Internet. How many feminists? That's not funny!!! How many thought police? None. There never was any light bulb. Mystery writers? One, but he screws it really slowly almost all the way in and then gives it a surprising twist right at the end.

under-cabinet lighting

I always thought that under-cabinet lighting looked impressive, like the bridge on the Starship Enterprise – far too good for the likes of me. But then I helped dismantle someone's kitchen units which were under-lit, and saw that the impression of technological sophistication was actually a hollow sham, easily accomplished by the laziest bodger. This was more my sort of thing.

All you need is a hole cutter for a spotlight or a screwdriver for a strip light. Many cupboards have some sort of fascia board so you can't see their bottoms; but if yours is showing, a strip of melamine (chipboard coated with white plastic, which your units are probably made of), inset from the front, doesn't look too vile. I went for recessed spotlights, which meant buying an 8-centimetre hole cutter, a marvellous bit of kit that fits onto your drill and is perfect for cutting 8-centimetre holes, though not much use for anything else. It makes a lot of mess, but the spotlight went in perfectly. I ran some flex through a hole in the back of the cupboard to a plug socket, put a plug on the flex, and plugged it in. I didn't have the guts to leave the back of the bulb bare, poking into the cupboard, like a proper bodger would have done. Instead, I built a safety box: five panels, 3 inches square, stuck together with No More Nails glue. This not only protects the bulb but also acts as a plinth for special tins of soup.

The effect is slightly impaired by having to unplug the kettle first, but then one flick of the switch and it's warp factor nine please, Scotty.

moving a socket

Interfering with electricity will result in certain death. That was the message I learned at the Science Museum as a small child when my parents took me to the Big Bang artificial lightning display, which has since been discontinued on mental health grounds. But our recent kitchen reshuffle meant I had to move a socket because in its former position it represented a potential hazard.

The theory is simple. Turn off the mains and get out your bludgeoning implements. With my hammer and heavy bolster chisel I bashed a channel in the plaster, 3 centimetres wide, along the neatest (non-diagonal) route to the new position, then smashed a hole for the socket box. I also bought a blank plate to seal off the existing socket, some heavy-duty 32-amp cable, and a sheath to hold it in the wall. Even with the mains off, I felt like I was operating on a lightly anaesthetized rhinoceros.

Triple-checking the power was off, I unscrewed the plate of the existing socket and beheld the wires inside. They reeked of death. I took a deep breath, unscrewed the three terminals, and inserted the stripped ends of my flex (sealing the existing socket with the blank plate). I ran the sheathed flex along to the new socket box, screwed it into its crater, wired up the plate, then sat back in contemplation of what I had done. Then I went out and enjoyed a cup of tea.

Now that I'm back, darkness has fallen. I suppose I will have to turn the electricity back on. Wish me luck.

hiding wires and cables

Modern electronic gadgetry looks so slick and convincing that even when it goes wrong you tend to blame yourself. However, that aura of invincibility is somewhat diminished by the terrible mess of cables that are needed to supply it.

If you are lucky enough to have an alcove with at least a dual plug socket in it, you can sometimes bunch your electronics into it by installing fitted shelving. Each shelf has to have a little notch in the back for the cables to run down to the plug. If your equipment is a snug fit, then make the shelves detachable so that you can get things in and out more easily. If the shelves need to be permanent, make the notches at the back big enough to accommodate a whole plug, because it is very annoying to have to take the plug off something before you can get it out.

For speaker cables, most people use cable clips and run it along the top of the skirting; but if you have stripped floorboards there may be a gap under the skirting, formerly filled by the carpet, into which the cable can be wedged. If you are keen, you can get down on your hands and knees and chisel a small trench into the plaster, or else lever off the skirting and run the cable behind it, but these are quite drastic options that can open up a whole World of Bad. Plus, there can be no, 'Mmmm, I think I preferred them where they were before.'

Me? I just know those high-tech product development guys have got the whole cable thing covered, so I'm waiting until they invent a completely cordless system. Come on, guys. Hurry it up.

fitting a doorbell

Doorbells come in two parts: the button and the actual bell.
A signal needs to pass from one to the other, usually by means
of a wire, activating a small noise-making device which tells
you that you need to creep up to the spyhole and decide if
you want to open the door.

Drill a small hole into the door frame, pass the bell wire
through the hole, and then strip off the rubber insulation.
Bell wire is particularly fine as it is for very low voltages,
which makes it fiddly to strip. For instance, if you are using
the wire cutters on a pair of thin-nosed pliers, you will probably inadvertently chop the end off a few times before getting
the hang of it. Hold the pliers open and press the wire into
the jaws of the cutter, rotate it slowly and deliberately, then
pinch off the sleeve of rubber.

Once you have wired and positioned your switch, you
need to find a good place for the bell – near a plug unless it's
battery-powered, and somewhere you can hear it from a long
way away. The best doorbells are radio-operated with a range
of up to 120 metres and flashing lights for the hard of hearing. You can take them into the garden and they will still alert

you if you're mowing the lawn or wearing headphones.

I had to destroy mine because my neighbours liked it so much they all got one. For a while, if you rang at numbers twenty-seven to forty-five on our street, everyone came to the door. You can programme them for different frequencies, but they always seemed to find out which one I was on and tuned to it.

fitting a video entryphone

Some people think video entryphones are illiberal, a bit Big Brother, and that screening visitors via CCTV is the beginning of a continuum of self-aggrandizement and paranoia at the other end of which sits Blofeld, stroking his white cat and plotting global destruction.

Unlike many grand schemes, this one comes with an instruction booklet, which says that first you must sort out

Blofeld: CCTV pioneer.

the power. Luckily, we've got a spare plug in the Surveillance Room. I mean, the hall. I ran the flex along the skirting with little flex staples, though one day I'll dig a channel and conceal it (yeah, right). Eventually, I may even wire it into the mains following the simple diagram at www.entryphone.co.uk. But don't hold your breath. I stapled 40 feet of coaxial wire (the TV aerial stuff) along the shortest route between the door of our flat and the front door of the house, and then through a hole in the door frame. This connects to the camera, which I bolted to the wall outside the front door: around 1.65 metres is a comfortable face height, but you may want to make them stoop or stand on tiptoe for your amusement. A length of electrical flex also connects the handset with the front door, powering the release mechanism.

A chair has now gravitated to beneath the handset and the temptation to press the button to see what's happening on the porch as you pass by is too great. Soon, you don't pass by. You just watch, your face lit by the eerie glow of the screen. Swap the white cat for an ancient, flatulent Staffordshire bull terrier and it's almost uncanny. Today, my porch. Tomorrow . . . who knows?

fixing fairy lights

Fairy lights have always been a mystery to me: how they work, why they sometimes don't work, and why anyone mends them when a new set costs less than £10. My brother has healing hands with electrical devices so the way to fix fairy lights in our family is to invite him round for a mince pie.

But mending them is quite straightforward, apparently. If the strand is dead, they're probably wired in serial – that is, one after the other – which means if one goes, they all go. Parallel-wired sets don't go out if one bulb fails. Check each bulb in turn by replacing it with a good bulb. Eventually, you'll replace the bad one and the lights will come on – unless there are two faulty bulbs, in which case this approach is useless. My brother (who uses his gift to heal mainframe computers) tests each bulb with a multimeter. You can buy a multimeter for about three times the cost of a new set of lights. Alternatively, you can use another working set of lights to test the bulbs, using one of its sockets to try out each bulb from the duff set. Of course, you may not have a fault: try tightening the bulbs to get them going, or get your screwdriver out and check your plug.

I got in the mince pies and my brother arrived with a colleague from the computer biz. They tinkered away and it all seemed to be going well until I foolishly sniggered at the fact that two men whose professional clients pay £400 an hour for their services were working on a £10 string of bulbs. They agreed this was ironic and left me to it. So this year I bought a new set.

TV aerials

Good television reception is something you take for granted – like the availability of Häagen-Dazs twenty-four hours a day at the all-night garage, say. Until you don't have it. Moving house can have a disastrous impact on the quality of your vegetating hours if your TV reception is bad and couch food is hard to find.

It happened to me, moving into a dip in the landscape where the transmitter's signal didn't reach and luxury ice cream meant a Wall's Feast. Sooner or later, I was going to end up on the roof, in either a suicide bid or an attempt at better reception. I always think of Rod Hull when I'm up on a roof: that unforgiving slope seems designed for things to slide off – rain, DIYers, and famous comedians alike.

Getting up there was no problem: a roof hatch from the loft opened within 1 metre of the ridge. (If you don't have a hatch, you may have to hire a special roofing ladder with a crook-shaped hook that fits over the ridge.) I felt it was a tool-belt situation, particularly as I needed both hands to carry the 3 metres of metal tubing that would (I hoped) be sufficient to raise the aerial, butterfly-clipped to one end, out of the dip. Ideally, you should be roped up, but instead I edged out along the ridge on buttocks clenched with fear. I shuffled into a very secure position before drilling into the chimney stack, with a masonry bit, to secure the three brackets for my pole. Down-stairs, feet up and unwrapping my Mivi, I pondered the words that St Peter apparently said to Rod: 'Why not just get cable?'

going solar

I'm changing my electricity supplier – to the sun. A thousand pounds buys enough kit (from www.windandsun.co.uk) to run a fridge, television, computer, and a 60-watt lamp. You get two solar panels (3 foot x 1foot), a battery, and an 'inverter' – a silver box that converts the electricity from DC current (bad) into AC current (good). Then you just plug a normal four-way extension lead into the inverter and you're up and running. The best place for the panels is the roof, but the petty-bureaucratic council couldn't begin to contemplate such a thing. 'It's harmful to the appearance of the environment,' they said. So when the ice caps melt and the Thames is flowing down the street, that's OK so long as the rooftops aren't desecrated with solar panels.

The panels, basically two sheets of glass with a layer of photovoltaic cells in between, come in a sturdy aluminium frame, and I got mine working as they leant against the garage wall. I could have just left them there but instead I made a wooden frame, which tilts them at the recommended 30–40°, in an unshaded part of the garden next to the house. This meant I could run a normal lead through the wall. But if your panels are any distance away you should use armoured cable, buried deep under the lawn to prevent a spade accidentally slicing through it. Mine is a small 'stand-alone' system, not yet able to sell back surplus energy to the grid (which they are obliged to buy), but it will grow. And when it does, at the first opportunity I'll be sending them a red bill demanding that they pay up within twenty-eight days.

improvements

It's only natural to want to improve your surroundings, but it's also solidly practical from an evolutionary point of view because it will enhance your survival and reproduction prospects. Keeping the rain out is good, but showing that you have the time, resources, and creativity to enhance your environment with an extra shelf or two has probably always helped your pair-bonding prospects, man or woman. Surveys reveal that women still buy men power tools at Christmas, but probably more in hope than expectation.

laying a lino floor

When I discovered those scuzzy carpet tiles that are coarse enough to graze your skin if you slip on them but are fairly easy to clean, I was delighted. Perfect for my scuzzy kitchen, I thought, and at about 15p each they did raise the tone for a while. Until they became irrevocably soiled. In key spillage areas around the cooker and fridge they were replaced so often that I stopped glueing them down – but that is not the flooring tip I wish to bring you now.

I recently helped a friend (dead posh graphic designer) lay a cheap vinyl tile floor and I learned much in the process. I screwed 6-millimetre plywood over the floorboards and reached for the lino adhesive, but was waylaid by several days of filling and sanding between the boards until the surface was, frankly, ridiculously smooth. We started laying tiles in the middle of the room, working outwards so the awkward shapes would be less visible, but I retired when it became clear I was outclassed. I trimmed tiles by eye, with a Stanley knife. She used a scalpel, cutting board, and steel ruler. Her tiles were perfectly aligned and putting-green flat. Mine looked more, er, organic.

Most important is getting the right notched spreader to dictate the depth of the adhesive. 'If you cock that up, it's a nightmare,' says my friend. Weighted down with copies of *Vogue* while the adhesive sets, the result is impressively expensive-looking. Which brings me to my flooring tip: if possible, get a graphic designer to do it.

jazzing up kitchen units

Kitchen unit depression is insidious – like seasonal affective disorder but all the year round. It has almost been proved in a number of studies that if a significant proportion of your kitchen is Swedish sauna pine, it can be seriously detrimental to your mental health.

That's why I ripped the doors off my units a couple of years ago, hoping to do something with metal instead. The trouble is that there are so many options with metal. If you send £80 and your measurements to www.gecanderson.co.uk, they will send you a pre-cut, stainless-steel panel to glue over your existing door. They send the glue, too. But my doors (Formica effect with aluminium trim) were not suitable; besides, I'd already burned them in a classic display of kitchen unit anger, so I would have had to make new MDF doors and the steel still wouldn't have gone round the edges. The same company will wrap your existing doors in steel, or make new ones, which is no use to me.

A cheaper metal is zinc, sold in 8-foot x 3-foot sheets from roofing suppliers. Armed with metal-cutting scissors and a lovely zinc bender, you can treat zinc like fabric and cut out a pattern and wrap your doors yourself. (Check that you have standard concealed hinges; butt hinges mean cutting an ugly notch in the metal.) Take the doors off and, one foot at a time, bend the sheet carefully around them with the bender. Gently beat the edges flat with a mallet or panel-beating hammer (leather- or copper-headed) and, when you're happy with the fit, glue with Unibond PVA adhesive and it will never, ever, come off.

One friend made a frame, stretched the zinc like a canvas, and punched holes through it in what she described as a 'Mexican design'. Not bad, actually. Now I have kitchen unit indecision, bordering on kitchen unit depression again.

tackling limescale

Limescale is more than just a brown-white stain on your sink and a gritty taste at the bottom of your tea. It is a stain on your character, evidence of your own sloth measured out in geological time. Limescale is caused by a gradual accumulation of mineral deposits in tap water, showing that whole rivers of water must have passed over the affected surfaces since you last cleaned them. It's also bad for your health, trapping bacteria and increasing your risk of skin infections and other minor ailments.

After years of neglect, my stainless-steel kitchen sink was beige, almost completely encrusted with limescale. The draining board looked like a dry riverbed, and a small stalactite had formed on the end of the tap. After snagging my hand on this for the hundred and fiftieth time, I resolved to make the sink shine or get a new one. There are many anti-limescale products available (including tablets for the kettle, which work perfectly); £8.95 bought me a litre of a caustic liquid, called HG hagesan blue, which claimed to be 'a marvellous product to remove limescale'. And so it was. The directions said to apply it with a sponge, but I poured it on and watched it fizz first. It also said to 'avoid contact with skin', though I tend to think that if it doesn't hurt at the time it can't be that bad, so I didn't bother with rubber gloves. As a result, I am still nursing painfully dried-out hands three weeks later.

But hey, there's no limescale on them.

clearing outside drains

Drainage may sound unglamorous, but it is one of the things that separates humans from beasts. From the first cities of Mesopotamia to the Tokyo harbour reclamation scheme, the idea of conducting effluents and rainwater away from where we live has given us the dry ground we needed underfoot to come up with the silicon chip. So, if one of your outside drains is slow to clear and prone to overflowing, don't think of it as something you can put off indefinitely; think of it instead as the beginning of the end of civilization, at least in your immediate vicinity.

Run a hose into any suspect drain until it 'backs up' and you have a nice pool of water to stick your arm into. Gather an audience if possible; small children are usually particularly impressed by what you are about to do. Remove the grate and roll your sleeve up to the armpit. Wear a rubber glove if you like (but it will almost certainly splash over the top). Stick your arm into the murky water, perhaps up to your biceps, and feel around for anything blockage-like. You may find a small dam of twigs, leaves, and silt, rotted into slime, but be careful dismantling it as it might contain sharp objects. Retrieve as much debris as you can before it is swept away to become another blockage somewhere less convenient. If the water doesn't suddenly drain away, probe with a bent coat-hanger. If you're still flooded, then hire drain rods.

The most important thing to remember is to work your audience. Tell them just how disgusting it is down there and slap anything vile you find theatrically down in front of them. But don't pretend to get caught by the Drain Monster or the little ones start to cry.

draught-proofing

With the wind whistling through our flat like the icy blast through a yurt on the Mongolian tundra, it is winter inside as well as out. It is better to draught-proof in the winter, I find, partly because you have more incentive, but also because you can tell where the draughts are coming from by the blue marks on your children.

Big gaps in floorboards – even the big one in the kitchen through which we can eavesdrop on the flat below – have to be plugged with beading (thin strips of wood). Usually, this comes in bleached white pine, which takes a stain well and can be blended to match the surrounding wood – if you can be bothered – though it's easier to decide to make a feature of it. Shave it to fit, wedge it in and secure with wood glue where necessary. Clear mastic, applied with a gun, is great in older houses where nothing is aligned properly and a dollop of white might be conspicuous. A £2 roll of insulation tape can stop near-storm-force gusts getting through around window and door frames – don't be afraid to double it up to get a really tight fit.

Feeling yourself actively plugging out the wind can give you a warm surge as you contemplate the reduction in your heating bill, but all that warmth has made me ponder the extra dust mites I will be supporting. Forty-seven different species (eleven just for bedding); ten million in a mattress; 20

per cent of the weight of my pillow. Apparently, they don't like draughts. Or Mongolian tundra.

hanging a heavy mirror

A big mirror can double the size of a room – though preferably not by bringing down the partition wall. Mirrors are perceived as shiny, friendly objects, but if they break they can become a cascade of blades raining down on your vital organs. I recently salvaged two enormous mirrors: one was already mounted on MDF, which made it heavy but safe (now leaning, chained to the wall); but the other was a wobbling, flexing sheet of potential harm. Carrying it upstairs, I stared Death in the face and saw that he looked exactly like me, only worried.

The flash way to hang a mirror is to have a glazier drill holes in the corners and then use 'mirror screws'. But my mirror was too big for the glazier's drilling table. When I suggested improvising with trestles, he said: 'If it flexes and the drill catches and spins it, we're dead.' He sold me Hodgson's Mirror Adhesive. Can a single tube really support 50 pounds

of mirror? 'Of course,' he said, with the confidence of a man who would never have to sit on the toilet wondering if a large mirror was going to fall onto his head. 'Squirt fifteen blobs on the back, press it on, and step away.' The blurb on the tube was less confident, suggesting I also rest it on the skirting board, after reinforcing it with screws and chiselling in a channel to accommodate the mirror. I also screwed a mirror-sized sheet of ½-inch plywood to the wall to even it out, then applied the adhesive.

And now the bathroom, which used to look short and narrow, looks long and narrow instead. Hurrah.

replacing door handles

In Jean-Paul Sartre's *Nausea*, the antihero's mental disintegration is marked most starkly for me when his door handle becomes a giant maggot in his hand, bringing on the eponymous desire to vomit. I know exactly how he feels. I'm heartily

Jean-Paul Sartre:
'Hell is a bad doorknob.'

sick of my own living-room door handles and I resolved to do something about them last weekend.

The first obstacle is locating the grub screw, a small, often headless screw that looks like a larva (try not to gag), but also serves the crucial purpose of anchoring the handle to the spindle that turns the mechanism and so facilitates the whole door-opening process. This tiny screw is best removed with a tiny screwdriver because bulkier devices are difficult to manoeuvre in the overhang of an elaborate handle.

Handle gone, you'll find most spindles in the UK are British Standard (BS) 8 millimetres square, so your fashionable new foreign handles had better comply or you'll need to buy a new spindle, cut it to the right length, and wedge it into the 8-millimetre hole in the door using something very small and strong such as little slivers of oak. Most new handles come with their own grub screw, which probably won't fit the thread in your existing BS spindle so you'll have to go back to the shop and get a new one anyway.

This is still a lot less bother than descending into existential humanist Marxism. I went for an abstract organic-shaped handle, which feels a bit like a giant maggot. I think I'm going to be . . .

fitting an extractor fan

I was in my kitchen, surrounded by shiny components, having doubts about fitting an extractor fan. In between buying it and trying to install it, I'd also cracked a rib. At times like this, I draw inspiration from how they coped in Colditz, making false passports out of toilet paper and German uniforms from navel fluff.

I was trapped in the kitchen, injured, with only a set of instructions for guidance. Extractor fans come in two main parts: the hood (the bit that plugs in), and the flue cover (the tube that goes up to the ceiling), which is generally retractable so that it can adjust to any ceiling height. The hood is secured to the wall with two adjustable brackets (a moment's work with the drill), designed to let you lift it on and off easily – useful for getting it level. Fitting the flue cover, trying not to exert myself for the sake of my rib, I had to hold it with one hand while marking it out with the other. It slipped, slicing into my thumb and splashing blood onto the hood. Then the hood had to come off again so I could tunnel a hole in the ceiling with the 3-inch hole-cutter attachment on my drill. Then I gaffer-taped one end of some plastic ducting to the hood's extractor unit and fed the other end into the loft. Unfurling the ducting in the loft meant edging along a filthy joist on my belly, nursing my rib, where I felt real empathy with my tunnelling Colditz counterparts.

You can train the ducting out under the eaves, ideally fed outside via the soffit board next to the guttering. Or – as I did – let it lie in the loft. Finally, I fitted the bloodstained flue cover into place: mission accomplished.

repairs

As Robert Pirsig, author of *Zen and the Art of Motorcycle Maintenance*, lamented, it is sometimes difficult to alert people to the joys that simple routine repairs and maintenance can bring. Pirsig mentioned one friend who felt that motorcycle maintenance was just not part of her world: 'It's a whole different thing,' she said. 'Like garbage.' But maintenance of anything can vastly improve your quality of life – from emptying your guttering, which can prevent damp in your walls, to the warm glow inside that you get when a job is done and you know that you won't have to do it again for a long time.

filling a wall

Mick, as I think I have mentioned before, was a Clint-like figure. Squinting into his skinny roll-up, he had this way of just appearing, silhouetted in the doorway, with a puff of smoke. A proper guv'nor passes on his skills to the next generation and is present in spirit whenever his pupils practise those skills. So, whenever I apply Polyfilla, it is in the presence of Mick 'On And Off' O'Reilly, a Cockney Clint in white overalls.

'Clean. Your. Sodding. Tools.' was his first instruction. Cleaning your tools brings you into contact with the cold steel of the filling knife, which must be straight-edged and clean so it won't cause drags in the finished surface. Then sprinkle some powder onto a largish mixing board, make a trench with the handle of the filling knife, and half-fill it with water. (Top tip: one part Unibond PVA adhesive to four parts water equals much stronger filler.) Carefully chop the powder into the liquid.

Mick mixed filler like a kata, controlling volatile elements with precision. My first attempt caused a waterfall onto Mick's shoes, but we eventually got some onto the hawk (a board with a handle used by plasterers; make one with an 8- to 10-inch square of plywood and an offcut of two-by-one for a handle). 'When applying filler we use a technique called On And Off,' said Mick, squinting to make sure I was taking it in. 'We put it On like this' – squelching a dollop into the hole until it oozed liberally – 'and then we take it Off' – deftly skimming the excess to leave a perfect facsimile of the wall. 'On and Off. That's how you remember it,' he said, passing me the hawk, now that I was fully trained.

Sadly, Mick is no longer with us, but his spirit lives on, and off, whenever I use Polyfilla.

restoring grouting

When it was new, our grouting attracted unsolicited praise from a satisfied user of our bathroom. 'Nice grouting,' he said. It was. A series of crisp white avenues, drawing out the subtle greys, blues, and browns of the tiles. These days it looks more like a grid of ditches criss-crossing mudflats.

With a visit from the in-laws imminent, I decided to restore the grouting to its former glory. And not with any of those temporary measures, like grout renovator, which you paint on, then wait six weeks for it to go brown again. A grout stick is another quick fix that I will not be using, for similar reasons. This time I will re-grout properly, raking it out to a depth of 2 millimetres, sometimes tapping gently with a hammer, taking care not to crack any tiles as I go. Then I will choose a grout from our local tile shop.

'This is our bible,' said the Groutmeister, the man in charge of grouts, producing a book of twenty little metal channels of grout, from grey to green to black via yellow. I costed the operation at £15 for 5 kilograms of grout powder, plus £7 for the rubber-bladed squeegee to press it in with, plus about a thousand man-hours of digging out, mixing up, applying, and buffing with a cloth once it's dry.

Or, if you want a really quick fix and your guests aren't likely to use the shower, toothpaste, applied with your Homebase Spend & Save card, lasts the critical couple of days and smells nice and minty. Available mainly in white, though Sensodyne Gel does an acceptable aquamarine.

re-enamelling a bath

When some gormless electrician drops his pliers in your bath and chips the enamel, you have a number of options. Kill him and chop him up in the bath. Charge him for a new bath, go through the whole installation process, and then kill him. Or meekly buy an enamel repair kit and mend it yourself.

I took the last option, which involves the extra humiliation of not being able to use your bath for four days while the hardener sets. The instructions make it seem riddled with pit-falls, but it wasn't so bad. The hardest thing was mixing up the filler, at a ratio of 30:1 with the hardener. What does 30:1 look like? (And no wonder it takes four days to set, with such a tiny bit of hardener.) But I digress. The crater in my new bath, though conspicuous, was less than 1 centimetre wide and less than 3 millimetres deep, so I only needed a smidgen of filler (and what does a thirtieth of a smidgen look like, for heaven's sake?). Anyway, it dried hard enough for sanding in the allotted time. The instructions became daunting at this point. 'Please note: the quality of the sanding will determine the finished result.' So, no pressure, then. Actually, it was a doddle, but painting it meant making a stencil the exact size of the hole and spraying Alpine White from a centimetre away. Nerve-racking or what?

Amazingly, the mend is genuinely invisible, so I chose the right option. I had favoured the middle one, but I just couldn't bear the idea of reliving the whole nightmare over again. Having that bath installed was hell.

a creaking step

Creaking steps are a serious occupational hazard for midnight snackers like myself. It used to be that steps three, seven, and nine in my house were the ones to avoid, but when four, five, eight, and ten also began sounding like Dracula's coffin lid opening, I knew I had to act.

The first thing you need to do is get into position. For lower steps, which are accessed via the cupboard under the stairs, this can be a mission in itself. It is sensible to empty the cupboard completely so you have a clear view under every step. This also unearths long-lost household items such as warped tennis rackets, tins of hardened paint, and vacuum-cleaner bags for a different make of vacuum cleaner from yours. I burrowed a tunnel into this detritus, then edged into it on my back, armed with chalk, a hammer, and a bag of little wedges, honed earlier to match a template wedge removed from another step. The wedges hold the risers and the treads in position, and creaking is usually caused by them shrinking or becoming compressed with age. My assistant walked up and down the stairs, calling out the number of the noisy ones, which I marked with chalk. One by one, I hammered in my little stakes – they slot into the corners of the steps where they meet the wood of the staircase – silencing the Dracula noises for ever, or so I'd hoped.

Top tip: glue the wedges in place or they'll pop out again after a couple of weeks. So now I'm back to good old steps one, two, and six, and doing the dressing-gowned triple jump with my glass of milk every night.

damaged cornicing

Le Corbusier believed in the sanctity of the cube and wouldn't have had any truck with fancy cornicing – and he probably never had his girlfriend insisting he patch up a whole roomful of the stuff before she got back from holiday.

Like slabs of wedding-cake icing (which I don't like, either), our Georgian cornicing looked as though it had been picked at by a giant six-year-old bridesmaid. It was sufficiently florid to require professional help, so I took a small section to my local plaster moulder who, amazingly, found a match from stock. Six impressively white sections of cornicing arrived to fill the gaps in our greyish stuff, plus a ceiling rose like a big pavlova (which, as desserts go, I don't mind).

I squared off the gaps and scored the wall with a Stanley knife to make the adhesive stick. Cornice adhesive spreads with a filling knife, like yet more icing. Pressing each section

Le Corbusier had
no time for cornicing.

into place, I supported them with a couple of nails until the adhesive dried. After two coats of emulsion, no one would notice the joins, though they might notice the missing plaster sunflower, which, when I accidentally tapped it with a hammer, detached itself and smashed into a thousand pieces on the floor. Middle of the night, girlfriend due home. And then it hit me. Marzipan.

A few glasses of wine later and the missing flower was rendered in almond-flavoured confectionery, coated with Unibond PVA adhesive, and painted with emulsion. It's not perfect, but the eye isn't drawn to it either. There's a risk of mice, but if they can get up there, then good luck to them.

a broken window

Ours was a house with many windows, many older brothers, and many, many trips to the glaziers. Our record was four trips for one broken pane. The first broke in the car on the way back, the second blew over while propped against an outside wall (take heed), and the third cracked as my brother tapped in the last panel pin holding it in place. I still remember his dance of rage when he realized what he'd done. The fourth piece went in just before my parents got back.

First, kick out the rest of the pane – or, rather, carefully remove the larger pieces of glass and wrap them in newspaper sealed with tape. Stick tape onto larger panes in order to break them safely (or to kick them out). Then get your dad's chisel – I mean an old chisel – and take out every bit of the old putty right back to the wood, taking care not to gouge the frame. Stir your putty vigorously, reaming the tub with the putty knife. It's the only language putty understands – otherwise it sticks and never dries. Bed in your replacement pane – ideally a couple of millimetres smaller than the waiting orifice – with a thin smear of putty. When the glass is securely pressed into place, tap in four panel pins, one on each cross-member, ever so carefully.

Ever wondered what the flat bit on the back of a panel-pin hammer is for? It's for this. Position the pin a couple of millimetres away from the glass, at exactly 90º to the wood, and let the flat bit of the hammer actually rest against the glass as you slide it onto the pin. E-e-a-a-s-y does it. Then apply the rest of the putty assertively. Stand proud like a matador, but with your little finger out, and get right in there and bevel those edges. If it's an emergency you can apply a coat of primer/undercoat to the putty while it is still wet. Polish telltale fingerprints from the glass, replace ornaments and curtains to original position, then act like nothing has happened.

fixing roof tiles

Fixing a roof tile is surely one of the most foolhardy ways of spending a Saturday. Or is it? A loose slate could allow a strong wind to lift off your whole roof, and water penetration damage could cost hundreds if not thousands of pounds to repair. Plus, a roofer might charge a couple of hundred pounds to do you know not what up there – possibly cracking more tiles in the process so that he can be asked back. A case is building for edging out onto your roof yourself.

It's best if the tile to be replaced is within easy reach of a loft hatch, but if this can't be arranged then you will need to hire a roofing ladder. This spreads your weight across the tiles so that they don't break and, more importantly, hooks over the ridge of the roof to give a firm anchorage. Nevertheless, whenever you are working on a roof it is important to remember: don't die.

When you are in position, wedge up the tiles adjacent to the damaged one very carefully – an inch if you're lucky – and then a good yank with a slater's ripper will hook out any nails that may be holding the broken tile in place. These need to come out anyway in order to get the new tile in. You won't be able to nail in the new tile, so instead nail in an inch-wide strip of lead that finishes below the bottom of the tile and can be folded up to hold it in place.

People pay hundreds of pounds to go on adventure weekends that are less exciting than this, so that's even more money saved.

cracks in the masonry

There are people living in Dudley right now wondering how to repair cracks caused by earthquakes. But even in less exotic circumstances, masonry cracks should be addressed sooner rather than later. Left unattended, cracks allow water to seep into the wall. Then the frost comes, the water expands, and the crack widens. Then there's the damp, rising and penetrating, which can cause your house to rot away and fall down.

All this is preventable with just a masonry chisel, a pointing trowel, a wire brush, and some mortar. Mortar is sand and cement, which comes ready mixed in a 5-kilogram bag: just add water. Chisel out any loose rubble from the crack and give it a good going over with the wire brush. Mix the mortar, wet the crack thoroughly, then press the mortar firmly inside, making sure to fill it. Trim off any excess with the edge of the trowel. Make the sharp, corner shape by placing the tip of the trowel at a 45° angle to the joint, pushing it into the mortar, and then firmly running the trowel along the joint.

If the crack follows the line of the mortar, then the structural implications are generally not as bad as when bricks are split down the middle, which could mean you have subsidence. Or that you live in Dudley. Either way, get it checked out before you act. An alternative to mortar is a flexible mastic, which can be squirted into the hole and allows for further movement when it dries; though it doesn't look so good. Crack repair is often hidden by rendering, pebbledash, or stucco, which gives added security to the mend. Until the big one hits.

saggy ceilings

A sagging ceiling can be a serious risk to your mental health – both from the sheer physical risk of it actually crashing onto your head, and from simply having that faint but horrifying prospect hanging over you all the time. Wherever you stand in the room, there's no getting away from the fact that the ceiling might just be about to fall any second now.

Our sitting-room ceiling sagged like a cheesemaker's muslin – or a series of muslins, loosely stitched together in a Bedouin tent effect. It dragged me down; but even worse was contemplating the extraordinary mess that would be involved in pulling it down. (I once put my foot through a ceiling and discovered that a paltry 2-foot hole was sufficient to coat every single object in the room with a good half-inch of thick black soot.) And then, worse still, there would be the plasterers, which is like having pigs to stay.

'Just screw the plasterboard back up to the joists, fill it and paint it,' said Richard, a builder friend. 'Use drywall screws, mind.' I bought drywall screws and a screwdriver adaptor for the power drill. This transforms the drill into a tireless driver-in and whipper-out of screws. One screw every foot or so, following the joists, braced the ceiling up an extra inch or two. But the effect was not the porcelain-flat finish I had hoped for. Sadly, it looked more like cantilevered underwear on cellulite. So we had a plasterer in to smear a skim coat of plaster over the sitting-room ceiling, which now looks immaculate and is a weight off my mind. Though the plasterer's visit has stayed with me for quite some time.

renewing a felt roof

Renewing a felt roof was one of the first major DIY jobs I tackled, in complete ignorance, as a teenager, together with some of my equally ignorant friends.

One of our number insisted on wearing evening dress throughout, complete with tailcoat and white dress gloves. He was going through a phase (weren't we all?). Felt roofs are usually found on flat-roof extensions or sheds, but ours was on the main house. It was always leaking because an area of felt had perished, and when we ripped it up the plywood underneath was rotten too.

'Aarrghh! Spiders!' shrieked someone, and it was true. If

spiders (or woodlice) are a phobia, then felt-roof restoration may not be for you. We replaced the rotten wood with new marine ply, which we covered with 'underlay', a self-adhesive felt laid in slightly overlapping strips. We coated the overlaps with bitumen (gorgeous, tar-like, black stuff), and then the roofing felt went on (making sure we staggered the joins to avoid the ones in the underlay).

Then came the fun part, banging in clouts along the seams. A clout is a big-headed, galvanized nail which, as its name suggests, needs a good thump with a club hammer. I have to say I have never seen dress gloves worn for this task since. With the hi-fi blaring, a good time was had by everyone but the neighbours. In between tracks we could hear the phone ringing, but there was no point in answering because it was only them complaining about the noise. Good job my parents were away.

safety

Every year around seventy people die doing DIY in the UK, and as many as two hundred thousand are injured. Not all of these injuries are serious enough to require hospital treatment, but cuts, bruises, and scrapes are nature's way of telling you that you are doing something wrong: you must be if you're bleeding. Usually, you take a knock or pick up a nick when your attitude isn't right; hurrying is a big culprit. Just imagine some really irritating finger-wagging person saying, 'More haste less speed,' as you run your bleeding fingers under the tap – and slow down. Tidy up as you go, and, hey, let's be careful out there.

how to escape death by DIY

'What? Is there no escaping death?' These were the last words of one Cardinal Beaumont, optimistic to the end, who at least died peacefully in his bed, unlike the unfortunate seventy people killed each year doing DIY.

The Department of Trade and Industry (DTI) says that ladders are the single biggest killer of DIYers, so brethren, as you dust off your tools this bank holiday weekend, be warned. Don't avoid them altogether, else you'd never get anything done, but don't take them for granted either. And never trust a ladder you haven't used before. I once put my foot through a rotten rung a few feet from the ground; if it had been higher up, I'd be a DTI DIY statistic by now.

'Doing DIY can be fun and saves money,' says consumer minister Melanie Johnson, 'but, before starting any job, you need to weigh up whether it is something you can do or whether you need to call an expert.' Sound advice from some-one who almost certainly calls that expert every time. Last year, there were 2,506 power-drill accidents (wear goggles, even for small jobs), 567 jigsaw mishaps (wear goggles and remember that the main action is underneath where you're cutting), 878 incidents with grinders (goggles, leather apron, and cricket box), and 1,920 errant circular saws (as an A&E doctor once advised me: 'Don't buy a circular saw').

So be careful out there, and try to escape that ignominious epitaph of death by DIY. Ultimately, of course, even if you subscribe to *Staying Alive*, the quarterly of the Royal Society for the Prevention of Accidents, there's no escaping death itself.

ladder tips

Tall ladders are scary. Climbing my first 9-metre triple extension, I felt the adrenalin; and once I was in position under the eaves of a tall house, the ground seemed a long way away. I wasn't tempted to overreach (the zone of safe working seemed to extend about 45 centimetres either side). But, as with most really big fears and concerns, I soon slipped into denial and after an hour or so of painting I nearly stepped back to admire my work. That jolt of total fear as I realized there was nowhere to step to has given me a lifelong respect for the tall ladder (though not so much the shorter, single-section one, which can sometimes be bounced along a few inches without getting down).

Ladder safety should always be paramount, however, and the two inviolable rules are: lean it at 70°, which means its feet will be about a quarter of its height away from the wall; and never go beyond four rungs from the top. If you need to go higher, get a taller ladder. Wear shoes with a solid instep; and make a work tray from an ice-cream box secured to a rung in front of you with coat-hanger wire, for tools and other things you might need.

Being up a ladder is a mixed blessing. You are in mortal peril and some discomfort, but are also less likely to be disturbed than when, say, working on a computer. Which is why your tray should be able to accommodate a packed lunch, thermos, radio, iPod, notepad, mobile phone, and a large sign reminding you not to step backwards.

avoiding back strain

Everyone knows the classic advice about avoiding back strain while lifting heavy objects: back straight, bend at the knees. But how many of us actually do it? It's such a silly posture to adopt, hunkered down but bolt upright with your bum sticking out, particularly if anyone's watching. So much less embarrassing to slip a disc and have your audience help you lie flat on the floor while someone calls an ambulance. Or is it?

Here's that silly posture in full, complete with tactics gleaned from years of inflicting irreparable damage on my own back.

1) Size the load mentally. Can you really lift a 50-foot triple-section ladder by yourself?

2) Clear a proper path so you are not negotiating children's trikes, etc.

3) Practise some grips. Cookers and fridges are designed specifically to cut into the fingers of anyone trying to lift them, so wear gloves.

4) Take a balanced stance with your feet about a shoulder-width apart, then squat next to the object, keeping your heels off the floor. Get as close as you can so that, as you lift the

object, it is against your body.

5) Try to grip with your palms, not just your fingers.

6) Lift your head, tuck in your chin, and straighten your neck, then lift the object gradually using your legs, abdominals, and buttocks.

Kneeling for long periods (painting skirting boards, gardening, picking up broken crockery after a row, etc.) can also strain your back because your knees hurt so much that you twist into an awkward posture to alleviate the pain. So wear knee pads.

how to prevent fires

I came downstairs the other day to find the kitchen ceiling obscured by a fast-moving carpet of smoke coming from two small fires: one in the fuse box, the other in a puddle of molten plastic underneath it.

Both fires were saucer-sized and getting bigger. Obviously, I ran around like a headless chicken for a bit, gradually circling in on the fire extinguisher. I'd been meaning to read its instructions for months but had always felt life was too short.

Now, I realized it soon could be. As my life flashed before me, I remembered that plastic fires can often be extinguished by blowing really hard. Amazingly, this worked. The incident prompted a major trawling of fire-safety tips.

1) Get a smoke alarm and test it regularly. Culinary cock-ups shouldn't be your sole means of testing.

2) Practise escape routes. We worked out that one of us might have to throw the baby to the other: we didn't practise that bit.

3) Check the sofa for a BSI kitemark, otherwise you may find it's made from kindling and stuffed with oil-soaked rags.

4) Get a fire extinguisher, and stash it away from the ironing board as these don't behave well in an emergency.

5) Don't smoke: smokers are statistically much more likely than non-smokers to go to sleep holding a lit cigarette.

6) If your smoke detector is beeping, replace the batteries as soon as you can be bothered.

After our incident, I felt a sense of achievement: all those lazy childhood days spent burning plastic soldiers into hideously deformed figures had not been wasted after all.

how to deal with asbestos

The Greeks used to weave asbestos into hankies, handing them out in theatres for the audience to cry into. At the end of the performance they were cleansed by fire for reuse, ensuring the maximum number of fibres circulated into the maximum number of lungs. It wasn't until the 1960s that a link was found between asbestos and cancer.

I once found a grey, fibrous panel over my fireplace that looked like hardboard but turned out to be asbestos. Panic. The council told me to pay for an expert to remove it. I phoned the HSE, which referred me to the Department of Health, which returned me to the HSE, which recommended the DTI, which sent me to the DTLR (the Department for Transport, Local Government and the Regions). 'Ask the HSE,' they said. Still, everyone agreed that if you have asbestos, and it's in good condition, don't disturb it. I

Aristotle may well
have sobbed into
an asbestos hanky.

unscrewed my panel, sticking gaffer tape over the seams to catch any dust, which is basically what the experts recommend. 'If you must drill into it, dab a blob of wallpaper paste over the spot to absorb the dust,' says expert, Steve Shutler.

There's no home-testing kit for asbestos, so the only way to find out for sure is to send a piece the size of a postage stamp (and £40) to someone like Steve (www.shutlers.co.uk), using the wallpaper-paste method to extract it and sealing it in a film canister. My council tip refused to accept my panel. 'It's dangerous,' they said. It's enough to make you vote in a local election. Almost.

smoke alarms

Smoke detectors are like sonic mines, designed to throw out a signal so piercing that you hear it whatever you are doing. Setting one off accidentally could easily kill you if you happened to be up a ladder and forgot what you were dealing with. So don't smoke while you're installing it.

Your chances of surviving a fire are three times greater if one is fitted – and working. Which is where I go wrong.

I hate loud noises, so testing it (standing next to it and pressing the test button) requires a long-handled broom and earmuffs. And the 'battery low' beep annoyed me so much I broke the detector while swiping at it with said broom.

Most detectors are held in place with one or two screws. Each floor should have a working smoke detector on the ceiling in the middle of the hallway or landing, at least 30 centimetres away from walls and lights. If you have a TV in a bedroom, put one there too. For the deaf, vibrating pagers can be worn during the day, and at night a vibrating pad goes under your pillow. Strobe lights are also available (rnid.org.uk/equipment), but they're more expensive than noise-emitting alarms; financial help may be available (though not for the merely irritable).

The Euro Meridian (secureone.co.uk) covers even the worst-case scenario: teenage children playing music that's too loud/indistinguishable from the alarm, only encouraged by the strobe light. No worries. It can text them. Ktcn's on Fya.

the carbon monoxide test

Before you turn on your central heating this winter, bear in mind that carbon monoxide (CO) officially kills seventy people every year – though CO alarmists (of which I am now one) believe this is a tenth of the true figure. Almost scarier is gradual poisoning by CO. According to www.carbonmonoxidekills.com, possible symptoms include: headache, nausea, vomiting, muscle pain, joint pain, dizziness, vertigo, numbness, memory impairment, word-finding problems, word-order problems, word-problems order, memory problems, anxiety, tearfulness, apathy, lack of motivation, memory problems, balance problems, tremor and memory problems. That's me! The website advice is cool, calm and collected: go to the doctor and get a blood sample taken. 'Go directly from your house, don't go elsewhere, as the CO in your blood will deplete and may not be picked up.'

Due to apathy, tearfulness, and lack of motivation, I couldn't be bothered, but I did call CORGI, the register of gas fitters, who said that yellow in the flame of my gas cooker meant a CO risk, but an all-blue flame didn't mean it was safe. And it's not just gas – anything that burns produces CO.

CORGI advises getting appliances checked annually by a registered engineer (www.corgi-gas-safety.com) and buying a CO detector. The Health and Safety Executive (HSE) found only one that worked properly for more than a year: the SF350. It's too big to wear as a pendant, but it will fit on your bedside table.

the truth about MDF

Where would we be without MDF? All my clothes would be on the floor, for a start. People associate MDF with TV makeover shows, and that's because it's so easy to use. Made from softwood sawdust and lots of glue compressed under heat, MDF is easy to cut, drill, and paint, and even an imbecile can produce serviceable, durable structures with it. And many have done.

Oh, the happy hours I've spent in my loft with a jigsaw, watching its fine dust swirl in the shafts of sunlight that peek through the occasional gaps in the roof tiles (must do something about those. One day). Then the rumours started. MDF is carcinogenic, they said, and it's banned in the USA.

My mum rushed round with a World-War-Two-style face mask as soon as she heard I was using it.

So, how bad is it? The main problem is the formaldehyde in the glue, which can seep out for up to three years after manufacture, increasing the risks of asthma and nasal cancer. Technically, all Californian homes built after 1988 should display warning signs. Formaldehyde seepage is reduced when MDF is painted; but when it is sawn, the airborne dust particles are perfect for transporting formaldehyde into your airways. Despite this, us plucky Brits are less jittery about it than Californians. The government says: 'It makes sense to use a suitable dust mask and work in a ventilated area or outside.' The DTI couldn't tell me whether my mask was up to standard, but I'll definitely be wearing it from now on. Even in bed.

pests

Getting rid of pests seems more like a call to arms than a call to DIY, though both operations benefit exponentially from proper planning. But there is something murderous, ruthless, and slightly alarming when you are called upon to eliminate entire populations of creatures from your property. But it's them or you, you have to tell yourself that. Mice, though a welcome indicator that rats are not present, are themselves unhygienic. Wasps are dangerous in large numbers near the house, and moths attack your curtains and your livelihood, by eating your work clothes, as well as your favourite jumper. If that's not over the line, what is?

combating moths

People who hate moths tend to be obsessive in other areas, I find. I know three moth-obsessives, all of whom could also be described as neurotic, fastidious, self-absorbed, clothes-conscious hypochondriacs (as well as smelling of mothballs).

Obviously, traits on that list, like 'clothes-conscious', exclude me, but I do own a suit (classed as 'business equipment') and any species that deliberately targets it as a food source comes into conflict with me. I could get a bat (echolocating, not cricket) and enter into symbiosis: it would silently eliminate moths at night and by day hang next to my shirts. But this would require some organization. Or you can place a bowl of soapy water beneath a lamp, attracting moths like, well, moths to a flame, then the soapy water drags them down. I prefer to use an actual flame in the form of a candle, though if your house burns down please don't write to me. Cedar, available as oil, chips, blocks, balls, and drawer liners is a classic repellent; and moth eggs are killed by tumble-drying and dry-cleaning, which also removes perspiration, crumbs, and other potential moth attractors.

I warned my snappy-dressing friends that, for safety's sake, hypochondria should always be the dominant neurosis, and that all insecticides are suspect. Imagine my enormous pleasure when the key mothball ingredients, naphthalene and paradichlorobenzene, were recently withdrawn from sale and declared to be carcinogens in high doses. The HSE has reclassified them as 'highly toxic; not to be used on clothes; do not inhale', etc.

Hypochondria is the one to remember, every time.

dealing with mice

I quite like mice, so I was actually pleased to see a little furry face peeking out from the top of the cooker when I flicked on the kitchen light in the middle of the night. I was fetching a glass of water, he was foraging on splashes of bolognese on the hob, and for a moment we looked at each other, equally startled, him probably more afraid than me. Then, with a twitch of his whiskers, he was gone.

Sadly for the mouse, the other occupants of the house did not share my benign attitude. My neighbour from downstairs, though in other respects a normal man, does a passable impression of the maid from *Tom and Jerry* if he sees a mouse. A week after my first sighting he came bursting up the stairs, metaphorically jumping onto a stool and squealing for Thomas. It was looking bad for the mouse. The council quoted £67 to make three visits: 'To assess the problem, then lay and collect the traps.' Depending on what they found, they might use poison or 'sticky traps'. These I didn't like the sound of. That little feller with the furry face getting his feet stuck to the spot until he starved to death? That wasn't going to happen under my floorboards.

The pet shop sold me a humane trap, called a Trip Trap, a plastic box you bait with 'something smelly, like peanut butter or bacon'. Or bolognese. The first night I tried his favourite sauce he was caught (like any great detective I felt I knew my quarry almost better than he knew himself). But where to release him? The park, to be caught by a cat or a rat? Camden Town Tube, to join his subterranean brethren scurrying between the tracks? Or should I take him back to the pet shop where I bought the humane trap, to see if they want to put him with the mice they feed to the snakes that they keep upstairs?

eradicating woodworm

If only they could be trained to bore vertically, woodworm could be harnessed to live in symbiosis with humans as a lazy, ecological alternative to drilling. As it is, because of their haphazard boring habits, woodworm are considered a scourge and are killed in their millions every year.

Admittedly, if left unattended they can seriously damage your house by spreading into hard-to-reach, expensive-to-replace structural timbers. So, if you do find any telltale holes (1–2 millimetres in diameter) in woodwork, tackle the problem sooner rather than later.

Any DIY shop will sell you some anti-woodworm juice, but find out whether it's water- or solvent-based: it's good to know if you're working with something highly flammable. Sometimes you get a squeezy plastic bottle with a pointy nozzle, and sometimes an aerosol with a plastic tube attachment. I pushed one of these down a hole and pressed the button. Immediately, froth poured out of the adjacent holes, followed by several flea-like adult woodworm which writhed for a bit, then lay still. I gave it a couple more squirts until the bunker was flushed out, and moved on. The tunnels all link up

beneath the surface, so only squirt every couple of inches.

Apparently, seeing adults is a rarity, as the larvae pupate for up to three years and the holes are made by adults boring their way out. So it's the babies you are killing. The babies in their nests. Sadly, woodworm have so far proved untrainable and so the senseless slaughter continues. DIY: it goes right to the heart of life's tough compromises.

ant control

Legendary biologist Professor E. O. Wilson recently published a book about ants, a species that, along with termites, makes up a third of the Amazonian biomass. The book, *Pheidole* (that's ants) *in the New World*, is nearly as heavy: an enormous

Professor E. O. Wilson
knows a lot about ants.

tome, sixteen years in the writing, which includes five thousand drawings by the professor himself.

Yet Wilson's ant opus has one glaring omission. He doesn't say how to get rid of them. I can put that right, as I was recently inundated by ants in the kitchen: swarming in armies large enough to reduce a small biscuit to crumbs in a matter of hours (actually quite handy for cleaning up little spillages: why wipe up a dollop of jam when you know it will be gone in two hours?).

Pacifists might like to try alternatives to poisoning ants. Wilson discovered that ants communicate using pheromone trails, so if you lay a sheet of A4 paper along an ant trail for half an hour, then rotate it 180°, incoming ants turn round and go back to the nest. This method works for just a few hours and would suit only pacifists working from home.

A mild bleach solution also disrupts their trails for a couple of days, but may spoil varnish and other sensitive surfaces. A bottle of bleach poured into the nest, however, usually does the trick. Or a tube of ant poison from your DIY shop. Forager ants take it back to the nest and feed it to the workers and the queen, killing them all.

In this age of CD-ROMs and digital photography,

Wilson's epic book is, by his own admission, 'the last of the great sailing ships'. And with my advice by way of 'erratum slip', now completely seaworthy.

tackling wasps

I try to avoid killing anything, but wasps long ago declared themselves an enemy species. I was put on notice when three of them stung me on the leg while I was carrying a tray of drinks at a barbecue. With my hands full, there was nothing I could do but watch (and shout, 'Bastards! Bastards!') while they pumped so much poison into me that I felt nauseous for hours. Bastards!

Suffice to say that when a wasp starts buzzing around me, I unsheathe my mighty 18-inch ruler and prepare to do battle. Our nest was just outside the back door and, recently, several wasps were milling there when a young buck headed over to check me out. The ruler scythed within an inch of him, then the backhand knocked him to the ground, and crunch, I squished him in half. Sting me at a barbecue? Hah!

But this is not the sensible way to get rid of wasps, and yes, I was stung by his friends shortly afterwards. The proper way is to call pest control at the council, who might charge to come out. But this was personal: so I went for chemical weapons from the DIY shop. I used Wasp Away, or Wasp Out, which comes in a spray can with instructions to use 'extreme caution' dealing with wasps' nests – advice I would reiterate, obviously. The blurb said to wait until dark when they were asleep, then stand 12 feet back and aim at the nest entrance. An arc of toxic froth poured out of the nozzle and into the nest. It felt like mass murder, but, with a baby in the house, this was self-defence. And tackling them one at a time with a ruler does tend to give them the upper hand.

the great outdoors

The great outdoors is a special place for DIY, where we rub up against our ancestral selves a little bit closer than we do when we are inside, and perhaps feel the call more keenly. Much more tempting, on a sunny day, to mend a broken fence with simple tools than to fiddle about inside putting up an extra shelf in a cramped bathroom. But outside greater dangers lurk, such as long ladders, slippery surfaces caused by rain, cold, biting wind, boredom, and loneliness. Which all make you appreciate getting back to the great indoors, the great DVD player, the great fridge, and the truly great quality time to be had on that fantastic sofa.

building a garden wall

As well as leading the nation in wartime, writing the four-volume *A History of the English-Speaking Peoples,* and being voted Greatest Briton of the Twentieth Century, Winston Churchill also did a lot of bricklaying, much of it at Chartwell, his country retreat. On a good day he could lay nine hundred bricks – or three times the number needed to get work as a bricklayer on site.

Consult a book of bonds (a kind of pattern book for bricks) before designing your garden wall, then cut bricks with a gentle tap followed by a firm one from a bolster chisel. The key to bricklaying (assuming you have marked out and dug a trench, and filled it with the right concrete footings), however, is buttering your bricks. Scoop up enough mortar to cover the end 3 inches of your trowel, then flick the trowel downwards and sharply back up again, so that some of the

Churchill laid a lot of bricks, but probably had very polite hod carriers.

mortar is propelled back onto the mortar board. The rest should now be stuck onto your trowel so that you can hold it upside down and it won't fall off. This is vital for buttering. Scrape a 1-inch-wide line of mortar around the edges of the brick that will abut the one you've just laid, to create a firm but yielding bed of mortar, then press them gently together.

Like Churchill, I, too, have juggled bricklaying with other careers, but even in my heyday I never came close to the great man's best tally. Though on our site he would have had to knock off at 3.45 p.m., endure tea breaks on the hour, and have the gaffer call him a fat bastard every five minutes.

repointing your garden wall

As winter approaches, the garden becomes less tempting, but think how it feels for your garden wall, facing the onset of frost, damp, rain, erosion, and intrusion by mosses all winter? If mortar gets loose, the edges of the brick become increasingly porous, developing visible holes that make them store water like sponges. When this water freezes and expands, it destroys the wall from within, like a million little woodcutter's wedges driven into an ever-increasing number of cracks.

Do your wall and your conscience a favour by chiselling out all loose mortar with a bolster chisel – get one with a hand guard, particularly if you are using a club hammer, which you will need if you are doing the whole wall. Mortar is no scarier than Polyfilla as it now comes in small 5-kilogram bags, ready to mix with water. Press it in liberally with the edge of your pointing trowel until a small surplus oozes out. Bevel this with the tip of the trowel so that, on the horizontals, the lower edge of the mortar is proud of the brick, to conduct away water. Do the verticals first, bevelling to the left or right, but be consistent. Trim off the excess with your trusty point-ing trowel run upside down along a straight edge (little finger aloft is optional, though only the toughest brickies do it).

This is proper 'weatherstruck' pointing, something to put on your CV and talk about at dinner parties. But how can you make sure it comes up? Your pointing trowel, properly cleaned, also makes an unostentatious cake/pizza/quiche slice (little finger aloft optional).

breaking up concrete

My fondest memory of breaking up concrete was doing it with a groom before his wedding. He was getting married at 3 p.m., but by 11 a.m. we'd already filled a skip and started loading a flatbed truck. There is something cathartic about breaking up concrete: it worked for Neill, soaking up the adrenalin of his big day.

It's also a peach of a job for a sunny day. You generally hire a skip, buying an exorbitant skip licence from the council; or you can buy builder's bags and give you and your car a hernia lugging them to the tip. Don't take too many bags at a time, and expect any family car full of rubble to handle like a Mini with a safe in it.

The key to this job is not to exert yourself. The big drill with the chisel bits you will have hired – probably a Kango or a Hilti – is very heavy and can kick the crap out of concrete. Find the tiniest existing cracks, rest the edge of the chisel bit along them, and press Play. The Kango will rattle your entire skeleton close to breaking point; but don't tense up and strain yourself. Or you could do what we did and throw yourself into it wholeheartedly, knowing that a night of feasting lay ahead. With our bones still buzzing, we made it to the church on time.

During the service, my eye automatically sought out small cracks in the masonry of the church. And I couldn't help thinking that we could have had the whole place down and in the skip and still made it to the reception for the best man's speech.

repairing flashing

Repairing your flashing might not be the first thing on your mind right now, but perhaps it should be. While we wallow in the dead time at the start of January, the outside elements have not slackened in their relentless struggle to enter our premises and cause thousands of pounds' worth of damage.

To keep out water, buildings are basically taped at the seams with lead flashing – the (often) zigzagging line of lead where areas of roof abut brick walls, like a porch meeting the front wall or a chimney emerging from a roof. You can pick up a roll of flashing at the builders' merchant's – or rather, you probably can't unless you go to the gym regularly since lead on a roll is uncommonly heavy. Add to your trolley a pointing trowel, a bolster chisel, and 5 kilograms of ready-mixed sand and cement. Use the old lead as a template to cut out a new piece (using a Stanley knife), long enough to overlap the joints. Dig out the old mortar, 1 inch deep, with the bolster and tuck the new lead into the groove, then roll up some off-cuts (like heavy cigarettes) and tap them into the gap every foot or so. Smooth the lead to the line of the roof and spoon in mortar with your shiny new pointing trowel.

Flashing needs to be done when it definitely won't be freezing, which is why it makes a good New Year's resolution. So sit back, pour yourself a drink, and if anyone disturbs you, say that you're planning some important DIY.

lighting a barbecue

As we evolved from herbivorous apes into omnivorous, hunting hominids, one thing became inevitable: the barbecue. The predatory behaviour of male chimpanzees in Gombe tells us that, long ago, females began selecting males who brought them meat, thus ensuring that aggressive hunters succeeded at the expense of gentler, sensitive types. And when

Homo erectus harnessed fire, the first celebrity chefs were born, and were incredibly successful with the ladies. A glimmer of this competitive spirit is still in evidence on suburban patios throughout the summer. Rusty barbies are retrieved from sheds and slaved over to produce meat charred on the outside and squirting blood on the inside.

Incompetence can often be traced to the fire-builders – usually sad, pallid men, who buy briquettes and bottles of lighter fluid, then wonder why everything tastes of petrochemicals. Barbecues are elemental, and primitive fire-starting methods such as rolled-up newspaper and small sticks, otherwise known as kindling, are required. Metropolitan men can hunt kindling in parks. You need only a handful, laid carefully over screwed-up sheets of the *Guardian*, to ignite your lumpwood charcoal. Don't start cooking until all the charcoal is white, turn food regularly, and douse any flames with a water sprayer.

All hail the hunters back from the supermarket with skinned chicken breasts and beers, ready to brave smoke in the eyes and salmonella.

putting up a trellis

A trellis is a versatile garden structure to which people turn at a certain stage in their lives. There is the kind that runs along the top of the fence, which 'adds height and is cheap and easy to maintain', according to one 'Vertical Gardening' website. Three trellis panels, together with a fourth on top, constitute a summerhouse, while free-standing panels covered with climbing plants act as screens, bringing you greater barbecue privacy.

One friend has recently gone for a full overhead trellis for the patio, featuring reluctant grapes inching towards a bitter wine crop of the future. Instant archways are also possible, though they should be handled with care so as to avoid looking as if you're constantly about to stage an outdoor wedding. The joy of a trellis is that it can simply be cut to size with a wood saw and then nailed to your existing fence posts or to other trellis panels, or to a 2-inch batten if it's going against the side of your house (to let the plants breathe and protect your wall from mildew). To do this, hammer-drill into your brickwork and fix it with screws and masonry fixings. A batten isn't a bad idea on a wobbly fence, screwed on to provide extra strength, where it gives something tangible to nail to.

Stand-alone trellis panels should be treated like a mini-fence and attached to posts sunk into concrete-filled holes, but make sure that all posts, fences, and trellis panels are strong enough to carry a heavy plant in full leaf (or even a fully ripened grape harvest), while simultaneously enduring the gale-force winds of British summertime.

laying a concrete path

Laying a concrete path is like putting down your marker in nature, imposing your will on your garden in a way that says, 'I will walk here when I like and have clean shoes at the same time.'

But, paradoxically, concreting over nature allows you to spend more time in it – particularly while making your path. First, dig a trench about 2 feet wide and 3 inches deep. May I suggest a curvy trajectory? Not wildly bendy or you'll just cut corners, but not straight to the shed or people will wonder what you are doing in there. Line the sides of your trench with 3-inch planks, held in position with stakes. For curvy bits, use 6-millimetre plywood. Use one part cement to two parts sand and three parts aggregate, all of which come in 50-kilogram bags from the builders' merchant's. The volume of path tells you how much to buy, so a modest 1 cubic metre path needs six bags of cement, twelve of sand, and eighteen of aggregate, enough to ruin the suspension on most family cars. Ask about delivery, or ready-mixed concrete, though these often have a minimum order size. Mix the dry ingredients in manageable batches on a board, then add water, just like a giant cake mix. Barrow the sludge to where it's needed. Skim it flat with a straight bit of two-by-one and leave to set for three days before removing the planks.

Obviously, over geological time, nature will win and your path will be swept away by some major tectonic upheaval. But until then, it's yours to enjoy.